The Isolation Room

Kenneth Toews

Copyright © 2019 Kenneth Toews

All rights reserved.

ISBN: 978-1-0918-2471-3

DEDICATION

This book is dedicated to my wife, Vicki.
She sought out good counseling help when I needed it,
but at the same time, pushed me to continue life.
Her love never coddled me, but encouraged me to overcome.
This book would not be possible without her.

CONTENTS

	Acknowledgments	i
1	The Game	1
2	The Room	6
3	The Retreat	19
4	The Schedule	39
5	The Escape	54
6	The Move	70
7	The Turning Point	84
8	The Prodigal's Father	100
9	Beliefs	112
10	The Past	118
11	The Importance of Truth	124
12	Just Like A Computer	148
13	Truth Replacement	152
14	Honesty	167
15	Anger: It's OK	175
16	Worship	183
17	Raindrops	194

ACKNOWLEDGMENTS

My thanks to Austin Reddington
for designing and creating the cover for this book.
You can see his amazing work at
austinreddington.com

CHAPTER 1

THE GAME

I had looked forward to this day for weeks. It was our annual summer family reunion, the gathering of a grandmother, six sets of aunts and uncles, and seventeen cousins at the family farm that my parents and I lived on. One of the uncles owned a barbecue chicken take-out business and he brought his big roaster and a whole slew of chickens primed for the cooking. Each year the menu was as good as it was predictable.

The farm was not all that impressive, only 32 acres, split down the middle by a single line of the Reading Railroad running only a hundred feet from the farmhouse. A row of climbable pine trees separated the front yard from a large meadow where a few steers that we raised for butchering grazed. Fields on either side of the tracks nurtured crops like tobacco, corn, wheat, and alfalfa. The corn and alfalfa were food for the steers, the tobacco and wheat provided supplemental income to my dad's factory job. The fields on the other side of the tracks bordered on a golf course.

The farm afforded bountiful opportunities and an abundance of room for the cousins to play. The focal point of our amusement was the two story barn. The first floor quartered several stable areas, a room for chickens, a utility room, and a plethora of nasty spider webs to dodge. I hated those things. I'm convinced that the first floor of our barn was a research and development lab for spiders to experiment with their web designs. They were all over the place. If I had to venture into the first floor of the barn for any reason, it was with great fear and trepidation. I hated the look of the spiders. I hated the feel of their webs just as much. The thought of tangling with a web gave me shivers. I fully expected them to release from the wall as I walked by and attack me.

As protection, the first thing I did upon entering was to grab the broom stashed just inside the door. I extended the broom out in front of me, moving it in a circular motion as I crept along to eradicate any webs in my path. I needed at least three feet of clearance on every side before proceeding. I ducked where I needed to and hugged the side of the walkways to put as much space between me and the webs as possible. When I reached my objective, I'd do my business as quickly as I could and return, almost running, to the outside following the exact same path, ducking and hugging in the same places. I was afraid the spiders might have a chance to re-spin their webs. It was such a relief once I got back to the fresh air outside the web lab. Every trip into the first floor of the barn was fraught with anxiety. If I had to do it again today as an adult, I'd still be using that broom.

The second floor was a different story (pun intended). It was one big open area with hundreds of recently harvested bales of hay filling in the tracks side of the barn. Earlier in the summer we had toiled, watering the alfalfa fields with our sweat as we relocated the bales from the field to the barn. Now at the reunion, we began moving those same bales around again, but this time it was for fun. We were fashioning a tunnel system. By removing a bale from the pile, we created a cavity, and laying that same bale across the top of the cavity produced a tunnel. Doing this a hundred times, creating cavities of various depths and sizes, and placing bales crosswise over those cavities resulted in a maze, devoid of light, complete with left and right turns, dead ends, split levels, and even a small room or two. Those who dared would navigate the complete darkness on their hands and knees, feeling their way through all the twists and ups and downs, with the goal of literally seeing the light at the end of the tunnel.

Barns do not have central air, not even a window unit. The sun's persistence on the tin roof generated thirst-inducing temperatures as we worked our construction site. Occasionally we broke from our labors and ventured to the windows on the front side of the barn, after inspecting the area for spider webs of course, and surveyed the landscape. We could see all the family cars parked on the gravel, the little red chicken house, the grand oak trees, and the steers lounging in the meadow, peacefully oblivious to all the extra activity. But most important of all, we could see that just a few hundred feet away was the legendary castle, commonly known as the "farmhouse." Tales had been handed down throughout the generations of a mysterious room inside this castle called "kitchen". Tradition held that inside this fabled room were vast amounts of refreshing liquids christened "Kool Aid" and "Soda" which had doused the thirst of many travelers.

The problem was that between us and the castle was a cadre of evil creatures (aunts and uncles), whose mandate was to protect the castle from intruders like us. Our clandestine mission was to invade the castle, maneuver our way to this magical "kitchen" and partake of the wonderful liquids that had satisfied so many before us, without arousing the attention of the beasts in the yard.

The operation required planning, cunning, and extreme secrecy. After a few minutes of conversation, a plan of action was established and off we went. First stop was the corner of the barn farthest from the house. From there it was a huge old oak tree across the lane big enough for two of us to hide behind at the same time. Next was a belly crawl along the grass to the fence that separated the yard from the meadow. We were confident that the blades of grass were adequate to mask us as we scooched along the ground. A quick climb over the fence landed us among the steers. They were useful for cover as we veiled ourselves behind their big bodies. We again belly crawled when we had to, being very careful not to belly crawl across a cow patty. Then it was the row of pine trees followed by a quick dash to the porch and into the door of the storied castle where the refreshments were awaiting.

Our mission was a rousing success and we were rewarded with tall goblets of cool elixir that relegated our thirst to the ash heaps of history.

While these undercover operations were a blast on reunion days with all the cousins, I also engaged in similar endeavors on my own.

I remember one evening in particular. I was alone in my upstairs bedroom. The second floor of the old farmhouse consisted of four rooms arranged in a square. Each room had two doorways that, as the English would say, "communicated" with the two rooms that adjoined it. The upstairs was accessed by typically narrow and steep farmhouse stairs.

The first room encountered upon ascending the stairs was one we called, for lack of a better name, the "middle room" because we had to go through this room to reach the rest of the upstairs. It contained my mom's sewing machine, a wall length bookcase for our encyclopedia, books, magazines, a closet, and a smaller bookcase where we stored our board games. The doorway to the right led to the bathroom. Straight ahead was my bedroom, and catty cornered from the middle room and between the bathroom and my room was my parent's bedroom.

One evening, I was in my room watching television. My grandfather, my mom's father, was working in the stairway. He was a painter and wallpaper hanger by profession, and he was replacing the wallpaper along the staircase.

Nature called, and I needed to go to the bathroom. For privacy reasons, I rarely travelled through my parent's bedroom, so my path to the bathroom necessarily took me through the middle room.

On this particular evening, my goal was to navigate to the bathroom and back without alerting my grandfather to my journey. This was not the first time I had taken on a mission like this, and it was more challenging than one might think. The problem was the farmhouse. Although it was well constructed, age had taken its toll. The floorboards were in the habit of creaking whenever weight was placed on them. This notified everyone in the house that someone or something was moving about and my goal for that evening was to secretly voyage from my room to the bathroom and back without a sound.

Having embarked on similar undertakings of this nature in the past, I had learned there were places that you could step that would not betray movement. I stood at the doorway from my room to the middle room, eyeing the location my left foot would land first. I took that step and repeated the procedure with my right foot. Cautiously, I maneuvered my way through the room, left foot, then right, some strides fairly short, others taxing the length of my legs. A few minutes later, I was back in my room, celebrating another successful mission.

The games children play. But there was one unique feature of this particular excursion. At the time it took place, I was not a child. I was twenty-one years old, and to me, it was no game. I was deadly serious.

CHAPTER 2

THE ROOM

I was watching TV once when a commercial came on urging people to adopt dogs who had been mistreated by humans. They showed a smallish, ungroomed, pathetic looking dog, hesitating as it stuck its head around a corner, and you could see it in its uniquely sad eyes. It longed to come toward the person running the camera, but was afraid to. It would inch its way out from behind a wall, but when only half of its body was visible, it retreated backwards to its protection. This happened several times. It wanted to come out. You could see the yearning in its actions. But past experiences produced a fear that overruled the desire for the companionship of the humans. I thought, this is a great picture of me as a teenager.

It was April of 1974 during my twentieth year of living when I commenced a full retreat from what is considered an ordinary lifestyle. My ambition was invisibility. I didn't want to be seen, heard, or noticed. In my mind, the world was better off not knowing that I even existed. I wanted to be left alone, and I wanted to leave everyone else alone. I welcomed solitude as my bosom buddy. It was the beginning of eighteen months of total withdrawal from people, a self-imposed isolation. I had checked out of life.

Except for occasional excursions downstairs, my cosmos was reduced to the four walls of my bedroom. It's where I ate my meals, watched television, and slept. That was the extent of my daily activities. It's about all I wanted to do. I had no desire to expand my horizons in the least. Any thought of venturing beyond my four bedroom walls was not only foreign to me, it also incited immediate fear and anxiety, and a certain discomfort in my stomach.

The Beach Boys recorded a song in 1963 called "In My Room." One line of the lyrics goes like this:

"In this world I lock out
All my worries and my fears."

Worry and fear were my forever friends throughout my teenage years. We were inseparable. They were faithful compadres that influenced all of my relationships, if you could call my paltry attempts at interaction with people relationships. Worry and fear were my barriers against any kind of meaningful communication with others.

Whenever I was in the presence of another member of the human race, whether the count was one or a hundred, self-directed questioning abounded. What should I do now? What should I say? What do they think of me? Am I living up to what they expect of me? If I do such and such, is that okay with them? I don't want to upset them. I don't want to look foolish. My whole life involved questioning what others thought of me, never just being myself. What I thought and how I acted was determined by my perception of what others wanted me to think or do. I was never just me.

I was the quiet, shy kid in school who never got involved in any of his school's social functions. I didn't attend my high school's sporting events even though sports was an interest of mine. I would have loved going to the games, but who would want to sit with me? You wouldn't find me at parties because I was the kid who never got invited. It tormented me that I wasn't included, but who would want me around when they were having so much fun? All schools have the kind of kids that just don't seem to have many friends because, in appearance at least, they are introverted and shy. I was one of those.

My bedroom became my haven where I could finally relax. The pressure was off because I didn't have to live up to anyone's expectations. I was alone and things were working out just fine. It seemed like a truce had been declared between me and my worries and fears. The conditions for the truce were that I would stay in my room, and in return, they would remain dormant.

One of the scariest times of my teen years happened at the ripe old age of 14. My church youth group went on a week-long retreat to Estes Park, Colorado. We were all really excited about it, even me. It was two overnights on a train from Lancaster, PA to Denver, CO, and then two more overnights back, with daytime stopovers in Chicago both ways. The trip didn't start out very well. This was June, and our train car for the first leg from Lancaster to Chicago had a slight problem. The air conditioning was broke and we sweated our way to Chicago, trying to sleep in straight-back seats that would not recline. It was pretty uncomfortable. But that would turn out to be the least of my problems on this trip.

Despite my reticence with relationships, I had become at least bearably comfortable with the kids in this group. I attended every Sunday morning, as well as most of the activities during the week, mainly because my parents went to church, and since they went, I went. My role in the youth group was as the resident bump on the log. I didn't contribute much, but I was there.

These were people I knew, people who I had deemed were not a threat to me. I needed the protection of familiarity. I had been with them enough to pretty much know my boundaries, their expectations, how I needed to act to be acceptable. I was under the assumption that I would be around my group the entire week we were in Colorado. Boy, was I wrong!

We had just arrived and were handed our dorm assignments. I went into shock. I was being separated from my group. None of the guys in my youth group were in my dorm. That was a possibility I hadn't even considered when I signed up to go on this retreat. If I had anticipated the slightest prospect of being split up from my youth group, I probably would not have gone. That scenario was just too scary for me. I would have needed some kind of assurance that I would always be with at least one member of my group, someone I knew.

But here I was, feeling like I had been ripped away from my security. I was relegated to a dorm building that was to be my home for the next week that now felt like the rest of my life. What was I supposed to do? Homesickness erupted. Fear exploded. Anxiety engulfed me. I was not at all ready to face an entire week in a strange place, among strange people, two whole travel days from the friendliness and assurances of home. The next seven days seemed like a mountain much larger than the Rockies which surrounded Estes Park.

I did the only thing I could do, and that's head to the place where I had been assigned. I must have resembled a lost puppy as I drug my sleeping bag and luggage into the building. I surveyed my surroundings. It was just one large room with rows of bunk beds. They might as well have been prison cells because I felt like I was incarcerated for the next week. I searched the room looking for the least threatening bunk I could find, one where I could be ignored. There were none. In my newly shattered world, every bunk had its issues. I finally picked a top bunk near a window, but in a corner against a wall. It was an area of the room that wasn't as yet heavily populated, and I was hoping for some buffer room between my bunk and the next inhabited one. I tried my best to look inconspicuous, to attract no attention from others situating themselves in their bunks, as I meandered my way through to the one I had chosen.

With anxiety still racing inside, I started unrolling my sleeping bag, continuing to act in such a way that wouldn't arouse attention. I wanted to be left alone. Mostly I wanted to turn around and go back home, but it was a long walk. I was stuck for the week. I was scared. Seven days from now was an eternity. How was I going to make it? How could I possibly get through this week? I would have given everything to go back two days when I was still at home in Pennsylvania. I was not at all prepared to be on my own around strange people. It was hard enough dealing with teenagers I saw at school every day. Now, every teen I saw presented a possible encounter with someone I had never seen before. How was I supposed to act?

I was feeling quite lonely as I settled in, but I wasn't alone long. Someone came in seeming to not have a care in the world and plopped his stuff down on the bunk beside me. So much for the buffer idea. He was the kind of person that exuded self-confidence, and what he did next freed me from much of the fear and anxiety I had been experiencing. After depositing his stuff, he turned to me and said "Hi". That's it. That's all he said, just a simple "Hi", but it somehow had a great impact on my outlook for the coming week.

He initiated the conversation, and just the way he talked, I sensed that he was not judging me, but just accepted me. He talked to me as if I mattered to him, as if I had some kind of value to him. All he said was "Hi", but that's all it took. Something about the way he said it seemed to melt away my anxieties. He took the initiative to reach out to me. It wasn't much, but it was enough to dispel my apprehensions about the next seven days. However, by doing this he had instantaneously become my emotional anchor.

He was a ninth grader from Manhattan, Kansas and stood a whopping six feet four inches. Just his demeanor and how he talked assured me that he was someone I could trust to not reject me. How I determined that from just a single, simple word is hard to explain, but for that week, he was my security. He was my self-confidence. He was my identity. He was my positive self-assurance. Whatever he thought of me is what I thought of myself.

Boy, did I latch onto him! For the entire week, I clung to him. I was the Joey in his Kangaroo pouch. I was the barnacle on his ship's hull. I was the rust on his old bike. He couldn't get rid of me. When he went to eat, I was hungry too. If he wanted to go play miniature golf, I was feeling athletic. At every retreat activity, I was right there with him. At the evening services, I made sure to sit beside him. When we went on sightseeing trips, I hung around to see which vehicle he rode in and made sure to get on the same one. I could never choose first because he might go to another one. After a couple of days, I'm sure he wished he had picked a bunk on the other side of the room. But I needed someone to cling to, someone who I could trust to not reject me, someone to be my social shield so that I didn't have to interact with others alone. That was my biggest issue at the time. I felt completely inadequate to interface with another person one on one. I felt that I had absolutely nothing to offer, and that if they got to know me, they would think I was a joke, a total dud of a person. I needed to have someone else in the mix that I could emotionally hide behind, like a child hides behind his daddy's legs when meeting a stranger. I needed a buffer between me and the others at the retreat. He was it.

Unfortunately, there was one daily activity that this buffer from Kansas couldn't help me with. That's when we broke up into discussion groups. Again, we were assigned to our groups. I genuinely loathed discussion groups because I had nothing to discuss. I had never formed opinions of my own because I always thought what I thought others thought I should think. Others gave me my opinions. God forbid that I should share an opinion on something and there be someone else who disagreed with me or asked me questions about it. I certainly couldn't defend my opinion because it wasn't mine to start with. I acquired it from something someone else said.

Discussion groups presented another problem for me. Because of my dearth of opinions, I really had nothing to share which led to me being mostly silent. But my intense preoccupation for what others thought about me also led to tremendous pressure. I was under enormous strain to share something, anything, even though I had nothing to say.

The week went something like this. Of course, there was the group leader who asked a question or made a statement to get the discussion going. I don't remember what the subject matter was this week, but we met every weekday morning. As usual for a bunch of fourteen-year-olds, things started out a little slowly and that was fine with me. No one wanted to be the first to speak, especially me, and it would have been awesome had we gone through the whole week in silence.

But invariably, someone other than the leader had to speak up, and soon someone else chimed in, then another, and another. Over the course of the first few days many had become involved in the discussion, but by Thursday there were still four or five who had maintained their silence. I was keeping count, literally. Every time another of the silent ones spoke up for the first time, I would mentally go around the circle counting who had shared and who had not. I was relatively comfortable when there were still a few who had yet to bestow their opinion. But as the number of participants increased and the pool of non-talkers shrunk, my comfort level started taking hits. Anxiety increased because I was sure that everyone in the group was judging me because I hadn't said anything. This is especially true when it was just me and one other person who hadn't broken our silence, as was the case by Friday.

I went to Friday's discussion group meeting highly distressed at the prospect that my comrade in silence might speak up. I kept watching that person, looking for any indication that they were going to leave me as the last of the silent ones. It was an excruciating vigil.

It finally happened. They said something. I was now the only closemouthed person in the group, and I was sure that everyone in the circle was as acutely aware of that fact as I was. There was no question in my mind that they were all looking down on me because I hadn't said anything at all for the entire week. My self-image was being bombarded. I was the scourge of the discussion group. The burden to contribute was overwhelming. I didn't know what to say, and I certainly couldn't just repeat the opinion of someone else in the group, but I felt like I had to say something.

After a number of excruciating minutes, racking my brain in search of something to share, I finally did it. I said something. I don't know what I said, and by the blank look on the leader's face, he didn't know what I said either. But the pressure was now off. After four and a half days of mathematics, adding and subtracting participants, I had spoken up. I had thrown that silence monkey off my back and I could now relax for what was left of that Friday discussion group meeting.

I mirrored the dog in that TV commercial. The dog wanted to come out from behind that wall to the companionship of the humans, but another internal compulsion told it to stay where it was. I battled between two forces: what I wanted to do versus what I felt like I had to do. I wanted to remain silent. On the other hand I had to say something because I thought everyone was denigrating me in their own minds because of my silence. The battle between the "want to" force and the "have to" force defined my life.

Perhaps nothing illustrated this more than my experiences, or lack thereof, with girls. I was a little more comfortable being around other guys, but only a little. At least we could talk sports and the conversation usually never got around to more personal things. However, girls were a completely different story. Girls were terrifying. They were the T-Rex of my Jurassic Park. If my life depended on having a meaningful dialogue with a girl, it was time to book the funeral home. I would not survive the ordeal. If through some strange twist of circumstances I ended up being alone with a girl, I couldn't put together two coherent syllables, let alone two sentences that made any kind of sense. Girls just turned me to a bumbling blob of buffoonery.

One girl in high school stands out. It's the stuff comedy movies are made from, but for me it was no laughing matter. She tried as hard as she could to get me to ask her out. She was giving me signs that Mr. Magoo would have seen quite clearly. As much as I wanted to, I just couldn't do it. My "want to" and "have to" forces faced off against each other daily.

We had an afternoon class together near the end of the day. I don't remember what the subject was. It doesn't matter. However, in my class previous to this one, I always sat close to the door so that I could be one of the first ones out when the ending bell rang. I'd hurry through the hallways to where the next class I had with this girl met. I wouldn't go in right away, instead I'd just stand around outside trying to look occupied with something, but always keeping an eye on the crowded hallway. When I saw her coming, my heart would start a-fluttering. I really liked her but I tried to look nonchalant, as if I wasn't paying any attention to her at all. My quick glances kept tabs on her location and when she reached a certain point, I made my move. I'd time my entrance to the class just one or two kids behind her, trying to act indifferent. I'd follow her into the classroom, let her pick a seat, and just casually sit within a desk from where she sat, again making every attempt to not look obvious. My goal was for my actions to look natural and unplanned, even though the same routine happened every day. Did I mention that I really liked her? The problem was, I couldn't do anything that might tip her off about what I was really feeling about her. I just couldn't be honest to myself or to her about my feelings.

Sometimes she'd turn around before class started and compliment me about something, anything, from my shoes to my hair. One glance at my high school pictures testifies to the fact that she had to stretch the truth beyond the breaking point to find anything good to say about my hair. It was shoulder length and a little greasy when I didn't wash it for a few days, which was the case more often than not. I never initiated any conversation with her, waiting, hoping for her to make the first move. I tried to act nonchalant to make it look like I wasn't thinking about her, but that's all I was thinking, yet I couldn't let my desires show.

She was kind of cute and I liked her, (or did I already mention that), and I knew if I asked her for a date that she would say yes. That was never a question. Everything she said and did around me was to encourage me to ask her out, but my fear paralyzed me. I "wanted to" ask her out, but I "had to" give in to fear. And so the war raged.

Every school day was a repeat of the previous one. My first thought upon waking up was a question – should I ask her out today? My immediate "want to" response - of course I should. She's trying to get me to ask her out. How stupid of me not act on the signals she is giving me! But then the "have to" force would kick in. But what if she says no? That would be horrendous. I can't risk that kind of rejection! On the other hand, what if she said yes? What do I do then? I would be a cluster of nerves until the fateful day of our date arrived. And then if we did go out and she got to know me a little and didn't like what she saw, what then? That's another risk I can't possibly take. The opposing thoughts would pound each other inside my head.

Since it was morning, my "want to" had a small advantage because our class together wasn't until the afternoon. Any decision I made early in the day didn't need to be executed right away so it was easier to pump myself up, muster up an adrenalin rush, and convince myself that I could do it. The moment of truth was hours away and it was easier to tell myself that today was the day when I didn't actually have to do it at that moment. It's easier to talk yourself into doing something a little frightening when the necessity for action is some time in the distance. As a result, my "want to" force initially gained the edge.

As the day wore on and the critical time approached, my resolve began taking hits. The "have to" force started making headway. The voices that spoke to me saying that I had to give in to my fears were now beginning to become shouts. By lunchtime, my willpower was transitioning into "maybe-power".

When it came time to enter the classroom, it was an even proposition. My internal forces were in a dead heat. Would I ask her out at the end of class, or would I back down? The thoughts overshadowed anything the teacher was saying. Throughout class, I went back and forth, back and forth, my thoughts pacing, wearing a path from one end of my brain to the other. I "want to" ask her out, but I "have to" protect myself and give in to my fears. I'd look at the clock repeatedly to see how much time was left in the class – thirty minutes, twenty minutes, ten, five, and finally one. My anxiety level ticked up with each second that ticked away.

The bell rang. It was time to leave. Here was my chance. I never had a chance. I chickened out each and every day. My "have to" force always won. I usually piddled around longer than I needed to gather my books together. While I was delaying, she got up and was out of the room before I was out of my seat. I had my excuse. She was too far ahead of me in the crowded hallway and I couldn't catch up. I manufactured the situation of having to gather up my books so that I would have a justification for not asking her out that day. This was the end result of the internal battle that took place all during the day, and especially in that class. My "have to" force would steadily gain momentum so that by the time class ended, it had overpowered the "want to" force.

I left school every day a little defeated, but also relieved that it would be another whole day before I was faced with the situation again. I went home for an evening of relative relaxation, but also beginning the process of hyping myself up for the next day's opportunity.

Ironically, what was probably the highlight of my emaciated teen social life involved this very girl. It was a

Saturday night and a friend and I, male of course, and really the only friend I ever did anything with, stopped at a McDonald's later in the evening to get something to eat. We walked in and I was startled to discover that this girl was there with one of her friends. My two forces immediately revved up. I was both excited and scared to see her there. It was actually quite a shock. It never occurred to me that I might run into her in my travels around town. If I had been alone, I would have tried to sneak out without her seeing me. I would have hustled back to my car, avoiding this random and potentially embarrassing encounter. But since I was with my friend, there was no turning back. We joined up to eat our burgers together.

Wow! What a rush! Here I was actually sitting with the girl who dominated my thoughts throughout the school week. It was tremendous. It was awesome. It's hard to describe the excitement I was feeling. I was actually doing what the other guys in school were doing and I felt like I belonged. I felt like a part of society at that moment. I felt equal to my fellow teens. It excited me to the highest of highs. I wasn't riding on cloud nine, I was straddling cloud fourteen. I can't overstate how emotionally satisfying this was to me. What others would call a trivial and commonplace event was to me momentous.

This moment of chance happened on a weekend night. I couldn't wait until school on Monday when I thought I would finally have the courage to ask her for a real date. Surely after such a positive experience I could finally overcome my fear and ask her what I had wanted to ask for months. What could possibly hinder me?

But Monday came and Monday left and I fought the same internal battle that always occurred on school days. Even though the memory of the weekend was fresh and kept impressing on me the excitement and thrill of it all and that there was no chance of being rejected, I had given in to the "have to" side of my feelings too many times. My "want to" was exulting in the victory of the weekend, but not enough to alter the outcome of another school day. I repeated the battles of the past few months, again with the same results.

After a while, I just expected that I wouldn't be asking her for a date. I never did. Sitting at home on the weekends watching television alone, knowing that guys I knew were having a great time on dates just killed me. Imagining that this girl might be spending date time with another guy was especially excruciating.

Loneliness became a constant and reliable companion.

CHAPTER 3

THE RETREAT

It was so uncharacteristic of me. I was scheduled to go with my parents on a tour of Israel in the fall of 1973. Instead, they decided to fight the Yom Kippur War in the Middle East and the trip was delayed until late January of 1974. Yes, traveling out of the country was uncharacteristic, especially after my experience in Colorado at the age of 14. But I would be going with my parents, and they were my emotional crutch on this trip. But that's not the atypical activity I'm talking about.

It was on this journey half way around the world that something happened that completely changed the direction of my life. I met a girl on this tour. Even more strange was that I didn't try to avoid her. In fact, we ended up hanging around each other for most of the trip. Maybe it was because the majority of people on the tour were older couples and also experienced matchmakers. Their efforts combined with the fact that we were the only two of our age in the group almost forced us to hang around each other.

Even stranger was the fact that she lived a mere forty miles from me and we started seeing each other after getting back home. As amazing as this sounds, we were dating! This was fulfilling on the one hand, but also alien to any experience I had ever had before. No, I didn't end up marrying her, but a conversation we had in a McDonald's one afternoon changed the direction of my life. It seems that every momentous occasion with a girl took place in a McDonald's. Maybe I should send these experiences to their corporate office. They could make commercials from them. But let me back up and relate how I got into this situation, and what exactly she said that changed my life.

Growing up, church was a ritual on Sunday mornings. It's just what we did. I grew up as an only child and every Sunday we deposited ourselves into the old Dodge and drove the twelve miles or so into Lancaster to go to church.

It was a Mennonite church, although not the kind you sometimes think about with the Mennonite denomination. There were no strict clothing regulations that some Mennonite churches adhered to. Dress wise, the congregation looked like any gathering of people at that time.

I don't remember much about the older man who pastored this church when I was younger. My understanding from what I have been told is that he at least believed and preached the Gospel. However he retired before I could really get the benefit of his teaching.

He was replaced by a younger man who didn't have the same commitment to the Gospel as the older preacher, and so his messages were more of the watery mush variety. We don't want to offend anybody, so we won't get into the nitty gritty of what God says in the Bible.

Because of the feebleness of the Sunday morning messages, my parents, especially my dad, were slowly losing their enthusiasm for this church. It was the Sunday when this pastor delivered a stirring and challenging sermon on the importance of making a will that my dad decided that it was time to move on.

I was a teenager by this time, and it was the youth group from this church that went to Colorado when I was fourteen. I always attended Sunday school and the youth activities fulfilling my role as the flower on the wall, and I was just as bored going to church as my dad was disillusioned. I got nothing out of it. But as long as my parents were going, so was I. That is, until I maneuvered my way out of the obligation.

When I turned sixteen, I got a car and a job. The job was at a local fast food restaurant that was just opening up. It wasn't part of a chain, but just a local place called "Huber's Hamburgers." They served the usual fare of a burger restaurant, only these had names like "Hefty Hubie" and "Big Hubie" which corresponded to McDonald's Quarter Pounder and Big Mac. There was a twelve foot tall cow at the entrance which we sometimes fastened onto a trailer and transported to surrounding towns for their fall parades. Our cow was one of the biggest hits of these parades because we threw out candy to all the kids lining the side of the street.

I was working on the very first day it opened for business. They started me out on the counter, meaning that I was the "may I take your order" spokesperson for the restaurant. It meant interacting with people, and I hated it. I was always afraid I would get a customer who was belligerent or unkind in some way. I just didn't have very strong people skills and I was easily offended. I was especially scared a customer might come back to complain about something. That kind of encounter really hit me where it hurt – in my self-image. I took things personally. Fortunately, I eventually worked my way back to the grill where I felt much safer, away from the danger of dealing with the public up by the cash registers. I was much more comfortable conversing with the burgers and buns than with people.

Of course, the restaurant was open on Sundays and I saw an opportunity that would give me an excuse to not have to go to church every week. I kept bugging the ear of the manager telling him that I would be willing to work the early Sunday morning shift each week. Many of the other workers were teenagers like me, and they were generally less than enthusiastic about getting up early on Sundays, especially after Saturday nights. After a few weeks I got my wish and was placed on the regular Sunday morning schedule. Now, when my parents asked me about going to church, I could honestly say that I had to work, even though I had essentially volunteered for the duty.

Shortly after this the young pastor delivered his spellbinding treatise on the importance of making a will that facilitated my parents' departure. They began visiting other churches and ultimately settled on a Grace Brethren church in a neighboring town that was true to the Bible and its teachings. They became members, but by this time, I was a well-established non-church goer. I was around seventeen and still had no interest in spiritual things.

It was October, 1971. I had graduated from high school, attended a technical institute for four months to learn computer programming, and was working for a hundred dollars a week as a computer operator at a local plumbing supply company. This is when computers were major works of art that took up entire rooms. I operated an IBM 360-30 whose CPU was housed in a metal cube about six feet high, three feet wide, and eight feet deep. That's what it took to do the job of today's chip that you can hardly see. How's that for a laptop? Also in this room was a printer about four feet tall, four disk drives, and four tape machines. Adjacent to the computer room on one side were two rooms where about twenty data entry people punched holes in cards, one card for each and every transaction of the company that day. On the other side was the storage room for all the tapes. All of this encompassed an area of about one floor of a good sized of a house.

I went to the technical school because I knew I couldn't

go to college. Sometime during high school, when I was still attending the Mennonite church, I went on a visit with the young pastor and his daughter to a college in Ohio that was affiliated with his church. It was here that I experienced a repeat performance of the Colorado trip. When I got there, I became really homesick, only this time there was no six foot four from Kansas to bail me out.

We arrived on Friday afternoon. I spent the entire weekend in the dorm room. The pastor brought meals to me, and all I did for two days was look out the second story window and watch whatever activity there was to see. I could not bring myself to venture out to socialize or participate in any of the weekend's activities. It was just too scary. I was simply too afraid to be around strange people. Confidence in myself was non-existent. This time, there was no one to hide behind so I stayed in the room.

We left on Monday around noon. That morning I was able to go to a chemistry class, and the only reason was because I knew that in a couple of hours I would be back in the car heading for home. Escape was imminent. On Saturday and Sunday, there was no looming rescue from the stress of being around people. I was stuck. On Monday, liberation was within reach. I knew that by that night I would be in my own room, sleeping in my own bed, and that gave me the courage that I needed to handle at least some minimal contact with people.

Because of this experience, I informed my dad when I got home that I wouldn't be attending college when I graduated from high school. The technical school was just a daily commute from home.

The computer operator job was a Monday through Friday situation. I didn't have to work on Sundays, but by this time my church attendance was no longer an issue. I didn't care to go, so I didn't.

My parents, however, were following a different path. They became heavily involved in their new church and my dad developed an interest in Bible prophecy. Books and pamphlets on this subject started showing up on the reading table beside his recliner, which I basically ignored, until one particular afternoon.

By now I was nineteen and had worked as a computer operator for over a year. I decided that another stint at a technical school was in order, this time the school was located in downtown Philadelphia, on Broad Street just a couple of blocks north of City Hall. It was a round trip of 140 miles three times a week. This necessitated an alteration in my work schedule, which allowed me to get off early on the three days that I drove to Philly for my tri-weekly night classes. The company was gracious to accommodate me.

I worked mornings on school days, which meant I had a couple of hours at home in the afternoons before leaving. During one afternoon of boredom, a little pamphlet on the reading table caught my attention. I'm not sure why it stood out to me other than the Holy Spirit was seeking me out. There was really no other reason for me to pay any attention to it at all. I was not interested in spiritual things. The title was "Ten Signs of the Soon Coming of Christ."

I have no idea who wrote it, nor do I remember all ten signs in the pamphlet, but three of the signs I read about that afternoon made an impression on me. First were two from the book of Daniel where Daniel was told to seal up the book of prophecy until the end times, after which two things that would highlight those end times were revealed. One was the increase of travel, and the second was the increase of knowledge. The third was from the book of Ezekiel where the return of the nation of Israel was predicted.

I put the little booklet down and just started mulling over the claims that I found in it. It struck me that the signs in the little pamphlet and what I saw actually happening in the world corresponded closely with each other. Were these really signs of the end times?

I can't say that this was a spiritual journey at first, although I'm sure God considered it to be just that. Initially this was just an intellectual exercise for me. I didn't know anything about sin and how it had separated me from God. This was an analytical workout, a scholarly exploration of the claims in this pamphlet, a question of academics. That's how I approached things as I thought about what I had read.

My own job verified the first of these signs, the increase in knowledge was indisputable. Computers were a relatively new development and were now doing the job that paper copies and filing systems used to do and had done for centuries. Mankind was learning new things about our world and beyond all the time, and at an increasing rate.

The surge in travel was undeniable. My grandparents lived at a time when muscle power, be it horse or human, was the only means of land transportation. The inventions of the automobile and airplane facilitated a huge spike in how far and fast people could travel.

The reality of the nation of Israel was also unquestioned. How many times has a nation been non-existent for two thousand years, and then been reassembled back inside the very same borders they inhabited two millennia earlier? Only one that I know of.

And that is how I started on my journey to salvation, by intellectually asking that if the Bible could predict these three events that were actually happening in the world, then could the Bible be true? Was this ancient book something that could have validity for us today?

I went to school that night puzzling over what I had read, and for the next few months I continued my cerebral exercise. I read other things on that table beside the recliner, including the Bible itself, but only when my parents weren't home. I didn't want them to know what I was doing.

Looking back, I understand that the Holy Spirit was working in my life, but at the time I had no idea who He was. I even began going to the church my parents had been going to and became heavily involved in the singles class.

If you asked me if I was a Christian, my answer would have been affirmative. I really thought I was a Christian because I believed the Bible to be true. There was no doubt in my mind about the veracity of the Bible. But my belief was a cerebral one, not a heart one, and I really was not a Christian yet, which brings me back to the fateful trip to Israel.

One of the authors my dad enjoyed reading was a man by the name of Nathan Meyer. He was a prophecy teacher, and sometime early in 1973 he advertised a trip to Israel for later that year. My parents decided to go and they asked me if I wanted to join them. The only time I had left the country was on short vacations to Niagara Falls and shallow excursions into Canada, and those were not always uneventful. My parents told me of a time when I was three years old. We boarded a boat to tour around the Thousand Islands. They said that as soon as we crossed over the border into Canada, I passed out and nothing they did could get me to wake up. They actually turned the boat around to go back to port, fearful of what might have happened to me. As soon as the boat landed at the dock, I woke back up. They couldn't explain it. I'm not sure if I was afraid of the boat, being out on the open water, or something else. It was a strange incident.

With my history of traveling, to Colorado and then to the college in Ohio, you'd think I might be a little hesitant to head across the Atlantic for ten days. As I said before, the difference was that I was going with my parents, and they were the buffer between myself and others. I had them to lean on. I wasn't alone and that made all the difference, so I readily agreed to go. There was little chance of being separated from them on this tour.

It was an overnight flight from New York to Paris that yielded little sleep, partly from excitement and partly from a fear of flying. As someone who can't swim and has a fear of heights, soaring over the Atlantic Ocean at thirty thousand feet for several hours was not very comforting. We had an eight hour layover in Paris highlighted by a guided bus tour around the city, during which I could hardly keep my eyes open. How frustrating to sit on the bus with a great view of the Eiffel Tower, Notre Dame, and the Louvre, and nod off every so often. I was so tired that it was just impossible to not fall asleep for a few minutes here and there.

After that semi-conscious day, we were back on the plane flying to Tel Aviv for a late night arrival, followed by an early morning start on our adventure around Israel.

Sometime during that first day or two, I started hanging around this girl, or maybe she started hanging around me. I'm not sure how it all really began. We traveled from place to place, walking together as we toured Holy Land must-sees like the Mount of Beatitudes, the Garden of Gethsemane, Calvary, and the Empty Tomb. It was quite exhilarating to sit beside her on the tour bus and walk beside her around the sights. I didn't have to manipulate any circumstances as with the girl from school. It was just assumed that we would be next to each other wherever we went on this trip. It was awesome.

For someone who always had problems maintaining a decent conversation, especially with girls, what was happening was even more remarkable. Maybe because we were traveling in Israel and there were so many new things to experience, I found myself able to hold at least cursory conversations with her. There was plenty to talk about without getting deep into personal stuff, things like Jerusalem, the Dead Sea, Masada, the Sea of Galilee, and the host of other sights in Israel. It was things like the blinding reflection of the sun off of the Dome of the Rock as we stood on the Mount of Olives overlooking the city, or discussing my fear of heights as we rode the cable car up to the top of Masada. It's a toss-up whether I'm more scared of heights or spider webs. It was easy to discuss how foolish we looked riding a camel. The rare four inch snowfall that fell on Jerusalem during the trip was a topic for discussion. The disgusting taste of a hamburger made from camel meat elicited unusually unhappy comments. The first bite of that burger never made it past my tongue. It was expelled before my teeth had any chance to chew on it.

Because we lived forty miles apart, when we returned from Israel we took turns traveling to each other's homes. This continued for about two months, but again, our conversations were never very deep or penetrating until this one fateful day.

It was March 21, 1974, a Thursday, one of those days when I had a free afternoon before embarking to Philadelphia and computer school. She had come down for the day and we were sitting at McDonald's eating lunch.

It was here that things started getting serious, not the relationship necessarily, but a question. She asked me point blank, "When did you become a Christian?" Uh-oh. How was I supposed to answer that? I was still in the habit of trying to determine how to answer questions based on how I thought the person asking wanted me to answer.

The question surprised me. It's something I hadn't really thought about. Of course, I didn't really do much in the way of thinking about things anyway. I had complete confidence in the truthfulness of the Bible. I was attending church every Sunday and heavily involved in the singles class there. At this point I did not doubt that I was a Christian, so I answered the question as honestly as I knew how. I said, "I just kind of grew into it." That's what I really thought. It was a process of coming to believe the Bible to be the Word of God and I was convinced that such a belief was all that was necessary to be a Christian. Again, I was thinking intellectually, not spiritually.

Her next statement sent me into a tailspin. She said, "There has to be a point in time when we must accept Jesus Christ as our Savior." By now I knew about how sin had separated me from God, but the idea of becoming a Christian at a certain point in time was foreign to me. I thought it was a process, a cerebral coming to grips with the truth. I'm sure that the church I was attending was teaching the necessity of a salvation experience, but somehow I had never caught wind of it for my life in particular. Well, that was the end of that particular conversation, but if was far from the end of my thoughts about it.

As I drove to Philadelphia that afternoon and sat through class, the impact of what she said was pounding away at me. My mind kept going back and forth, alternating between what I had concluded and what she said which argued against my conclusion. I kept saying to myself, "I believe the Bible completely. I believe God created the universe. I believe Noah survived the flood. I believe Jesus died on the cross for my sins. I believe there is an empty tomb. I believe Jesus is coming again. There is no question at all that the Bible is the Word of God. But what if she's right? What if I need to ask Jesus to forgive me at a certain time?" That was the mantra I repeated over and over probably a hundred times that evening. I knew there was never a specific point in time when I had become a Christian, and so the roller coaster of thoughts undulated in my mind.

I spent the three and a half hours of class not really learning much. These conflicting thoughts persisted. I could not rid myself of the doubts about whether I was a Christian or not.

As I got into my car at 9:30 that evening and headed west on Vines Street to begin the seventy mile journey home, I had to make sure. It was 9:37 PM, driving north on the Skukyll Expressway just outside of downtown Philadelphia when I asked Jesus Christ to come into my life. I'm not sure if I was driving or if the Lord had taken control of the vehicle. In any case, I was now sure of my status with God.

I sometimes wonder if this is not, at least partially, what Jesus points out in Matthew 7:21-23. There will be those who claim to have done work for God who will not make it into Heaven. How many of these people are there in churches today who were like me? They know the Bible is the truth, but they have never made a singular commitment to follow Jesus. A belief in the Bible is not necessarily the same as a commitment to follow Jesus. The demons believe the Bible to be true, but certainly have never made a commitment to follow Jesus. Intellectual belief is not enough. A decision to ask Jesus Christ to come into your life and live with you is the salvation experience. There might be a progression in the beginning to believe the Bible, but that progression is not enough for salvation. The progression must end with a decision. How many people in the church today will eventually hear Jesus say to them, "I never knew you; depart from Me, you who practice lawlessness," because they never made a decision.

Moving forward from 9:37pm on March 21, 1974, I could now say that there was a point in time when I became a Christian. My progression had ended in a decision. You'd think that the girl who steered me in this direction, the one who told me there needed to be a specific time of salvation, would have been happy to hear the good news. I'm sure she would have been excited, IF I HAD TOLD HER! But here is where the kind of person I had become got in the way. I never said one word about it and a few days later she broke up with me, I'm sure believing that she was parting ways with someone who was not a Christian.

What kind of person had I become? How did I handle this rejection? Let's take a look at one of my favorite TV shows of all time, the original Star Trek series of the 1960's.

The starship U.S.S. Enterprise whisked its way around the universe at incredible speeds. Its mission was to explore new worlds, seek out new life and new civilizations, to boldly go where no man has gone before. Some of these new civilizations were friendly. Some were not. Whenever the Enterprise encountered hostility, whether it be from the Klingons, the Romulans, or some unknown entity, one of Captain Kirk's first orders was to engage the ship's shields. These were electronic forces that encased the Enterprise with an invisible bulwark of protection to ward off aggressive acts on the part of whoever or whatever they were facing.

I had developed my own version of a shield of protection. Its purpose was to ward off the actions of whatever people or circumstances I was facing, mostly people. And it wasn't necessarily their actions I was trying to shield myself from. It was more concerned about protecting myself from my reactions to their actions, most notably, my emotions. This shield was my suppressor, my controller, that which censored any emotions that might arise from inside myself.

My hero from this show was Mr. Spock, the even keeled science officer from the planet Vulcan. Vulcan was a planet that had a bloody and violent history, to the point of self-annihilation. Wars were on the verge of destroying life as they knew it. The people of Vulcan preserved their planet by adopting a way of life that eliminated emotions and substituted logic in its place. In their estimation, emotions, especially anger, caused their violent history, and so logic was used to create a peaceful society. No more knee-jerk reactions. Instead a steady, methodical analysis of situations ruled their planet, bringing peace.

This philosophy of logic was music to my ears. To me, emotions were the bane of my existence. I remember being in a social studies class in high school. We were discussing, rather the rest of the class was discussing, economics and the stock market. The teacher asked us what we thought the major factors were that determined whether the stock market went up or down. At this point, someone blurted out an answer with some degree of noticeable anger. I looked around to see who it was and they were all looking at me. I, the one who didn't share, the one who didn't have an opinion, I was the one who spouted off an opinion. My outburst consisted of just one word, and that word was "emotions." It seemed to me that what the stock brokers were feeling emotionally dictated in great measure the movement of stocks that day. And I didn't just say the word. There was disdain in my voice, a definite aura of disgust that surrounded that word, emotions.

I hated emotions. I had no use for them. I didn't want to feel them, I didn't want to acknowledge their existence in my life. And so I used my "Star Trek" shield to keep them in check to the point of not even having any. The purpose of my shield was not just to keep others away from me emotionally. More importantly, it was to keep my emotions away from my own consciousness. I didn't want them, didn't need them, essentially, didn't have them.

When this girl broke up with me, I acted like it didn't bother me. My entire life to that point was an exercise to perfect the art of denying emotions. Since I was now a Christian, I transferred the denial of emotions into a Christian mindset, meaning that I shouldn't feel disappointment or sadness or other negative emotions. Christians aren't supposed to feel things like that because God is in control of all our circumstances, and feeling bad about something that happens to us is displaying a lack of trust in God. Negative emotions and a mature Christianity just cannot coexist. So I never felt grief or sorrow. I wouldn't allow it. My shield immediately squelched any attempt by my emotions to express themselves.

Here's the rub. There is a similarity between the protective shields of the Enterprise and my emotional shield. They both require energy to perform their duty. The Enterprise shield was not a naturally occurring emanation from the ship. It was, instead, artificially induced and required energy from the ship to maintain its potency. Likewise, my self-imposed shield also was not naturally occurring. God did not endow me with the inherent ability to suppress my emotions. It was my own creation and it took an enormous amount of effort to sustain.

Emotions are designed to be expressed in some way. That's just what they do. Of course, there need to be controls so that emotions are expressed properly and don't cause damage or hurt to persons or property. But to ignore them altogether, to pretend they don't exist, to keep them bottled up requires a shield that is alien to who God made us to be, and it can be exhausting to maintain. My shield required a certain amount of energy to preserve its effectiveness.

Also, if there was an attack on the Enterprise, the shields around the ship would weaken to a degree. A second attack would weaken the shield even further. Captain Kirk would divert power from other parts of the ship to the shields to keep them fully operational. He understood their importance and would do everything he could to keep them functional. Eventually, after a number of attacks, the shields would be completely gone exposing the Enterprise to the full potency of the next attack. Eventually, there would simply be no more energy left in the ship to maintain its protection.

This brings me to the events that led up to the onset of eighteen months of isolation.

It was a Monday, ten days after I became a Christian, April 1, 1974. It was during these ten days when the girl I met in Israel broke up with me. I was making preparations for my tri-weekly journey to Philadelphia and computer school. Shortly before it was time to leave I began feeling ill and was hit by a twenty-four hour flu bug of some kind, so I stayed home that night. This incident was the catalyst that propelled me into a year and a half holed up in my room.

My emotional force field was in full operation at this time, and it was embroiled in a war! This girl had just broken up with me and I refused to acknowledge that I should feel bad about it. The effort required to keep these emotions in check was quite taxing. Indeed, it was downright draining.

When I ended up staying home that Monday night, I

found myself able to relax mentally in a way that was so refreshing. I didn't have to put up a good front to my classmates at the computer school. I didn't have to act like everything was okay when it really wasn't. There was no one to make demands on me. There was no one to impose on me. There was no one to put on an act for. I was alone in my room. My mind was carefree, serene, tranquil. The bottom line was that I was able to just be myself, which required no effort at all. It was truly relaxing.

If it's possible for two organs of the body to have a conversation, the one between my brain and stomach might have gone something like this.

> Brain: "Hey Stomach. It's me, Brain."

> Stomach: "Hi, Brain. How's life treating you up on top of the world?"

> Brain: "Well, to be honest, it's been kinda rough at times, you know with the break-up and all. I'm tired. I'm not sure how much more I can handle."

> Stomach: "Can I do anything to help?"

> Brain: "Well, that virus we got the other night gave me a much needed break, and it also gave me an idea."

> Stomach: "What's that?"

> Brain: "It's like this. You know that whenever I'm around people, I have to keep this emotion shield energized. It tires me out. Being

home in our bedroom on Monday night was just awesome. Nothing to worry about, nothing to think about, I could just chill. What would happen if whenever it was time to leave the house, you could pretend that we might be getting a virus again. Maybe it would keep us home and relaxed."

Stomach: "OK. I'll see what I can do."

The result of that conversation was about two weeks of mental, emotional, and physical warfare. Every time I had to do something, whether it was going to work, to school, or even to the store, I got nauseated and wondered if I was going to be sick again.

I had two minds warring within me. My rational mind tried to reason things out, telling me that I was just imagining the physical sensations of sickness, and that I should ignore what I was feeling and go do my responsibilities. My other mind, the one that was weary of always having to suppress emotions, fought against my rational mind. It just wanted to rest, to escape constantly having to energize the "shield" to keep my emotions in check.

This back and forth debate continued for a couple of weeks. One time I even drove all the way to Philadelphia for class, but turned right around and went home because I just couldn't go into the classroom. Of course, just like the "want to" vs "have to" battle, I began giving in more and more to the part of my mind that wanted a break. Each time I gave in, it was that much harder in the next skirmish to opt for what my rational mind was telling me. My rational mind was getting weaker, while my "I need a break" mind waxed stronger.

It wasn't long before I quit going to school. I had to take a leave of absence from work, never to return to a job that I really enjoyed. My parents had me go through a series of medical tests to see if there really was a physical issue involved, but nothing was found.

I finally gave in. I quit fighting. I had run out of energy. The net of isolation drew itself around me until even stepping out on the front porch was a monumental undertaking. I just quit trying and resigned myself to a life within the four walls of my bedroom that worry and fear could not penetrate. I didn't see this as a temporary isolation. I was fully prepared to spend the rest of my life there.

In some ways, it was the easiest eighteen months of my life.

CHAPTER 4

THE SCHEDULE

He held up a picture, actually it was one of those "ink blot" cards that counselors use in their craft. It was one of the times some years after emerging from my isolation that I was seeing a Christian counselor during a season of particular struggle. He held up card after card of varying designs and scenes, none eliciting any response. Then he held up this one, and boy, did I react to it!

I can still see it clearly years later. It was a silhouette, black on white. A man was sitting alone in a room in what looked like a simple wooden kitchen chair. He was slouching with his legs extended straight out in front of him. From head to toe, his body formed almost a straight line. His hands appeared to be in his pockets. He was facing the only window. He looked at ease, or so it seemed to me.

The moment I saw this picture, I felt the pressure of a thousand elephants being lifted off my chest. It was a physical sensation and it was unmistakable. I experienced incredible weight leaving my body.

The message I received was this. Here was a man who was alone without a care in the world, and boy, was he enjoying it. There was no one around to tell him how to act, what to think, or where to go. He had no pressure to perform in any certain way. He was by himself, able to just be himself, and absolutely happy with the situation.

This is how it felt those eighteen months holed up in my upstairs bedroom. Gone were the worries. Gone were the fears. Gone was the pressure of measuring up. Gone was the mental weariness of sustaining my shield. What a great relief. I was enjoying an emotional peace and tranquility for the first time that I could remember. I was relaxed and happy.

My daily routine went like this. I woke up, ate breakfast, spent the morning watching TV game shows, ate lunch, filled the afternoon with Bible reading and verse memorization, ate supper, and watched prime time TV until it was time to go to sleep for the night– all without leaving the upstairs rooms. It really was a time when I had no expectations to meet, no standards to measure up to, no one pressuring me to act a certain way to gain their approval. It's hard to explain just how relaxing this was. I was free physically, mentally, and emotionally. No pressures, no worries, no fears, no shield, no expectations, no responsibilities, no wondering what I was supposed to do and how I was supposed to do it. It was wonderful. I finally had peace.

My life had always been a game of "twenty questions." Every human encounter was filtered through a sieve of expectations that I perceived, or tried to perceive, that the other person had for me. In my mind, every person I met looked at me anticipating that I would behave a particular way and it was up to me to figure out what that way was supposed to be. It was a guessing game.

I could never just act based on who I was. How could I? I never gave myself permission to find out who was inhabiting my body. Instead I always became the person I thought others wanted me to be. Freedom of expression was something completely alien to my experience. The pressure to perform was pervasive.

In actuality, the biggest issue I had was acceptance. I wanted to be accepted. I wanted to fit in. In trying to please, I was not scrutinizing my actions or words as much as I was making a judgment about my value as a person. Was I okay? Did I measure up? Was I accepted? If I was then I felt more comfortable being around. If not, then I wanted to retreat to a corner and hopefully go unnoticed. The question I constantly asked myself, was I worthy of their attention.

I played some organized baseball growing up. I was a decent defensive outfielder but a lousy hitter. They said I had a gold glove and a black bat, and my teams played like I hit. One year our record was one win against fourteen losses, the only win coming on a forfeit.

During one game, I came up to bat against a pitcher who had a mean curve ball. As I entered the batter's box, an alien sensation crept into my consciousness. It was a feeling of significance, of mattering. I was used to not counting for much, for having little impact in the lives of others. But here I was standing at the plate. There was the pitcher standing on the mound. I had a definite sense that he was paying attention to me. I was making a difference in his life. I was having an impact on him. He altered what he was doing simply because I was there. I was giving him cause to consider my existence. To me, this was a foreign feeling. I was used to not making an impression, having people look past me like I was invisible. It was normal to be ignored. But my presence in the batter's box was causing this pitcher to regard me as worthy of consideration, albeit not for very long. I struck out on three curve balls, swinging at one of them. But feeling like I was making even a small difference to someone else, no matter the length of time, was such a unique experience that it still stands out to me today.

This incident illustrates how much I felt like a nobody. For the most part, I was a non-entity in my own mind. I drifted through life like a tumbleweed in the desert, driven this way and that depending on the strength and direction of the wind. Never did I intentionally act based on a feeling of worthiness. I felt like I had nothing to contribute in any given situation and that if I wasn't there I wouldn't be missed.

I had no real goals in life. I knew of no real desires for my life. I would act based on what someone said, not based on any preferences of my own. What I desired was suggested by others. They did not originate within myself.

As a result, the need to analyze predominated my thinking. In any given situation I relegated myself to the background until such time that I could ascertain whether I was okay. Once I figured out what was expected of me, then I could move into a more inclusive role. I would pretty much need to be invited to a certain degree to participate in activities.

Example, suppose a group I was around decided to play a game, maybe dodge ball. I always wondered if they were including me in their plans. I could never just assume. Everyone would populate the two sides and start throwing the balls around. Should I just jump in and begin playing too? Do they want me involved? Would I be in the way? Sometimes I'd stand on the sidelines watching, and then edge on in, trying to not be too obvious that I was involving myself in the game. It would take someone acknowledging me to free me up enough to fully participate. For instance, if someone on my side had two balls and gave one of them to me, then I knew I was being included and I could begin to have fun with the others. Until then I just wasn't sure. I couldn't become involved simply because I wanted to. I had to make sure it was okay first.

This need to analyze my worth was predominant as long as there were people around, and since people were always around, it was a constant emotional exercise that promised no chance of relief. Now that I was isolated in my room that pressure was gone. I was alone with no one to burst my bubble of contentment. I didn't have to perform for anyone. I didn't have to wonder if something I did would cause someone to dislike me. I didn't have to perpetually question my actions, wondering if what I did was pleasing. I was having a wonderfully relaxing time.

Ninety-nine percent of my time was spent within a twelve by fourteen foot space. There were occasional ventures downstairs, but it was usually when there was no one else at home, mostly during the daytime when my parents were both at work. If my parents were at home, I would once in a blue moon hazard a descent of the farmhouse stairs for a brief visit and then head right back to my haven. Sometimes relatives or friends came for a Sunday afternoon visit. It was then that I "played" my clandestine games of secrecy, as I did when my grandfather was re-wallpapering the stairway. If I moved about at all it was very methodically, taking great care to not cause any noise that might alert the visitors to my existence. Even adjusting positions on the bed was slow and deliberate so as to avoid the revelation even the bed's creaking springs might cause. I didn't want anyone to know I was there.

Imagine what my parents must have been thinking about this time. Here I was, their only child, 21 years old, unable, or maybe in their minds unwilling, to leave the house. The very thought of departing from my sanctuary brought tremendous fear and anxiety, so much so that I eventually gave up all notions of the idea. I was holed up in the southwest corner upstairs bedroom, showing no signs of a life pattern change any time soon. I was quite content with my situation. For the first time that I can remember I was able to just chill and be myself.

However, there were practicalities of life to consider,

money being one of them. I knew I would have to earn a living somehow, but working at a job outside of the house was not an option. How could I leave my sanctum for an incredibly long eight hours a day to work around people? That scenario was not part of the equation. I had no intentions of changing my circumstances. I had no compulsion to change my circumstances. I was completely comfortable with the idea of spending the rest of my life in isolation.

I had a childlike naivety in my thinking. To support myself, I devised ways I could make a living without the inconvenience of leaving my room. This was long before there were ways to work from home. Perhaps because I came to know Christ through reading a pamphlet on prophecy, I thought about writing a book on the subject and supporting myself that way. I actually began writing about prophecy and I had delusions of people flocking to buy my book, thus giving me the money I needed, making it unnecessary to ever leave my humble abode. The book would have been a plagiarist's masterpiece had it ever been published. Oh, the bliss of ignorance. I never considered stepping out of the emotional comfort I was experiencing. Because I was so afraid to leave my house, my mind engineered all kinds of schemes that would allow me to support myself without having to leave the protective custody of my four walls.

My parents were good people. Their mild-mannered nature would put Clark Kent to shame. My wife and I joke about one of the biggest issues my parents had. Every time we visited them after we were married, this very serious topic of discussion surfaced without fail over a period of thirteen years. It was about whether to buy a ceiling fan for the living room. For thirteen years, they could not make a decision. It took over a decade of soul searching for them

THE ISOLATION ROOM

to finally get one.

One of our visits coincided with my mom's birthday. We were sitting around the kitchen table and it was time to mark the occasion. My dad reached around to the desk he used when working on the family finances. He pulled open a drawer and drew out an envelope containing a birthday card. He handed it to my mom. She opened it dutifully, read what was written therein, reinserted the card into the envelope and handed it back to my dad. He returned the card to the drawer where it would await the same date next year, at which time the process would be repeated with the same exact card.

As I said, my parents were good people. They would help anyone at any time with anything. They just were not communicative about the deeper issues of life, so when I retreated to my room, there was no track record in our family of penetrating discussions about serious topics. We just didn't know how to talk about the kinds of things that were broiling about in my mind. As a result, we never engaged in talks about my fears or worries. I was truly alone with no one to confide in. It's not that my parents didn't care. They just didn't know how to approach me, and so I spent my days eating, watching television, and sleeping.

Although my parents didn't communicate their concerns about what I was going through with me, they must have had conversations with people at church. This was the church I had begun attending prior to our trip to Israel. Someone in the church recommended counseling, suggesting one in particular that he thought might be able get to the bottom of my issues. This counselor's office was about thirty miles from our house, which would seem to be an epic task for me, a person who couldn't go downstairs without struggling. How could I possibly travel half an hour away from home to see some stranger?

Amazingly, it turned out to be less of a battle than it probably should have been. It was surprisingly easy to make the weekly to start, then bi-weekly trek toward Harrisburg. The reason, I think, is that I looked at this counselor as someone who could help me. Deep down, I really did want to get out of my prison, I just didn't know how. I was indeed helpless. I was truly in a hopeless state. There was nothing inside of me capable of engineering an escape. I had resigned myself to spending the rest of my life bound within four walls because I saw no other options.

Perhaps, I thought, this counselor could give me the directions to escape. Maybe he had the magic cure I so desperately needed. Was it possible that he had the keys to unlock my prison doors and free me to return to a normal life? I was placing my trust in him, and that trust replaced the fear at least for this one person, and that trust told me that I was safe with him.

For a year I made regular trips to his office. As usual, I never really thought through the ramifications of these half hour drives. What if my car broke down? Did it ever occur to me that I might have to leave my car on the side of the road to find a nearby phone? No cell phones yet at this time. What kind of panic would that have incited? I would have had to walk to a neighboring business or house, actually talk to somebody, and then wait around until help arrived. Hardly the kind of scenario that would bring me comfort.

Well, my car behaved and I saw this counselor for about twelve of the eighteen months of isolation, and I would like to say that I learned a lot about myself and why I was so fearful, but I can't. Responsibility for the lack of results probably rested with me more than with him. He asked questions, I had no answers. He asked me how I felt. I didn't know. He asked me what I was thinking. I wasn't. I was hoping he could tell me what was wrong. I didn't know he actually needed some information from me to accomplish his task.

Because I had no feelings that I would acknowledge, because my knowledge of myself was severely lacking, I really had no answers to give to him. I never talked about myself with anyone, and that included him. My answers to his questions were superficial and even nonexistent at times. I had no opinions. I did not analyze why I did things. I didn't talk about feelings and that didn't change during my sessions with the counselor. He was searching for clues about why I was so fearful and I had no clues to give him. I wasn't much help.

He tried everything he could think of, even hypnosis. He was a Christian counselor from a reputable school. He used the Bible at some point in every session, but perhaps because I was so little help in the conventional sense he decided to use hypnosis, hoping that would free up some of the secrets my mind had locked away. I'm not going to make a judgment about the use of hypnosis in counseling except to say that in my case, it didn't seem to work. I came out of the "trances" as numb and dumb as I was when I went in.

After about twelve months, the regular visits came to an end, but only indirectly because of the lack of progress. My job as a computer operator had paid a hundred dollars a week, not too bad, especially for an eighteen-year-old. And by living at home my bank account was fairly happy prior to my great retreat from life. As a result, I was able to pay the counselor's fees for a while. Over time my bank account became increasingly unhappy, the money dwindling down to the point of my dad having to pick up the weekly tab. However, a year of watching me make the trek up and back and seeing no signs of improvement took its toll. He decided that enough was enough. One week he gave me an envelope to give to the counselor, obviously a note saying that he was done paying for the sessions. Of course, I had no clue what was in the envelope until the counselor told me what my dad had written. Quite coincidentally on the very next visit, probably because I showed up without a check, the counselor told me that he thought I had shown enough progress to curtail the sessions. Of course, nothing was further from the truth. I was as ignorant about why I feared being around people then as I was on the first visit. And being as naïve as I was, I never made the connection between the note and the cessation of counselor visits. I simply went back to my room and continued my isolation from the world.

So it would seem that I was locked into my future, a future that promised very little. It was a future brimming with nothing. No friends, no goals, no desires, no motive to change, but still with no pressure to measure up, no need to energize my shield. Counseling hadn't worked and there was nothing to indicate that things would improve. But there was one activity I pursued during those eighteen months that I think was the catalyst for my eventual return to society.

Television was the only friend I really had and I spent most of my time soaking in all it had to offer. In the morning there were game shows. Late afternoon offerings were reruns of recent prime time programs. And in the evening I watched the best the networks could put out. But from noon until about four the only thing airing was soap operas. This was long before satellite and cable television and the four hundred choices those bring. Since I was a Christian, I had no interest in watching the struggles and naughty lifestyles of characters I didn't care about.

So after my game shows were done I turned the TV off and spent the afternoons reading, studying, and memorizing the Bible. I sent off for Bible correspondence courses that instructed me in the proper interpretations of what I was reading. For several hours each day I was ingesting the Word of God and I am convinced that this is what God used to strengthen me to eventually come out from the prison I had created for myself. I can't point to anything specific that effected my departure from my room, but I am sure that the Holy Spirit was working in the background the whole time to bolster me up so that when the time came to emerge from the shadows, I had enough spiritual conditioning to commence the journey.

One particular afternoon, however, does stand out. I was reading in Hebrews and I came upon chapter 12, verse 6 which says, "Whom the Lord loves, He chastens." I reacted to these words with an intensity that shocked me. Remember, I was Mr. Spock, for whom emotions had no place in life. Yet when I read those words, Niagara Falls had nothing on the water gushing from my eyes. My emotional constrictions had been penetrated and I began weeping uncontrollably.

The message I got from those words were quite simply, "I love you". That was it. Three simple words, but they struck a nerve that quiet afternoon. Just like the pitcher who payed attention to me when I was up to bat, here was the God of the universe also paying attention to me. Just the singular fact that God was taking notice of me flew in the face of everything I had experienced in life. I was the nobody, the invisible, the one of no consequence, the social delinquent. People who had no reason to ignore me, ignored me. Yet God, the One of the greatest significance, the Highest of the high, the King of all kings, the one and only Holy One, the One who had all the reason in the universe to ignore me, wasn't, even if His attention was in the form of chastening.

I somehow knew all along that I was under the chastening of the Lord. However, my view of God at that time was less than accurate to say the least. God was kind of distant, not very communicative, kind of involved in my life, but also kind of detached. His chastening was more of a duty than a desire to help. There was no encouragement, no "atta boy" moments, nothing but the unemotional necessity to fulfill what He had promised. Since I was now His child, He was required to take care of me. It was His duty as God.

Then I came across these words in Hebrews that said the reason I was being chastened is because I was being loved. They broke through, at least for that moment, the misconceptions I had about a dutiful, obligatory, unconnected God. The message was unmistakable and powerful. I was being chastened, therefore I was being loved.

Again, how amazing that the God who created everything that we see, who has all power, all knowledge, the God who is far above anything or anyone else that exists, this same God pays attention to a little person like me. It blows me away now and it blew me away then. Wow! Here was this great and all amazing God telling me that He loved me. The magnitude of this message overwhelmed me that afternoon and the tears began flowing.

Looking back, I can remember only twice when I heard the words "I love you". This was the second time, the first being as a child, maybe early elementary school age, and my response was entirely different.

I was laying on my bed because I was being disciplined for something. I don't exactly remember what I had done, but I've been told that my cousin and I were discovered one time by my grandmother playing in the middle of the street outside of our house, right on the double yellows. I'm sure we were having a great time on this road where the speed limit was forty-five miles per hour. I'm not sure how long our great time lasted before my grandmother saw us or how many cars with shocked drivers swerved by, but this could have been the reason for the discipline.

Be that as it may, as I was sitting on my bed, my mother came to the door, leaned against the door frame, and from there said that they (my parents) loved me and didn't want me to get hurt. She acted uncomfortable as she delivered these words. Remember, my parents were not ones to openly share things emotionally, and her demeanor as she spoke certainly affirmed that. She never entered the room, sat down beside me, put her arm around me or anything like that. She spoke those words from the distance of the doorway, maybe ten feet away, three or four steps, and then left. That was it.

Years later when I read 1 Corinthians 12:6, I reacted with a shower of healing tears. But as a child, I responded to my mother's words in a completely different way. Instead of maybe being thankful that I was loved, or allowing the words to ease the sting of being disciplined, I reacted by cringing. I recoiled like a baseball fan in the stands trying to avoid a line drive foul ball driven into the seats. I retreated like a turtle into his shell to protect himself from a dangerous enemy. Instead of accepting the soft, healing words that should have made me feel better, I rejected them. In my mind, my mother's words never had a chance. I couldn't believe that they were true. How could anyone love me? I'm not the least bit worthy to be loved. It's simply not possible to love me. I'm not good enough for that. All of these negative thoughts impressed upon my mind when my mother spoke words that should have helped restore me.

Why, at an early elementary age, did I feel like I was not worthy of love? Why was I fearful of interaction with people as a teen? Why was I horrified by the thought of talking to a girl? Why was a simple encounter with a girl at McDonald's so breathtaking? Why did I need an emotional "shield" to protect myself? Why did I finally hole myself up in my bedroom, prepared to spend the rest of my life there? Why did I want to just disappear and hope the world would leave me alone?

The simple answer is that I don't know. I simply do not know. There was no abuse, no molestation, no drugs, no infidelity, no skeletons in dark closets. No one woke up in the morning calculating all the ways they could "get Ken" that day. There were no sinister plots designed to hurt anyone. I don't have a testimony of how I overcame a terrible family history to become some great saint of God. Someone else will have to tell that story. Instead, nothing happened that was any more abnormal than happens in any other family.

But as an only child, with no siblings around to bounce things off of, I was left to interpret events as best as I could with the limited life skills of a child. My faulty interpretations led me down a path of retreat from others and repression of my own emotions. I learned to keep things to myself, and ended up perfecting emotional suppression as an art form.

Here's the bottom line. The first question that I asked a few paragraphs ago is really the foundation on which all the others were built. Why did I feel like I was not worthy of love at such an early age? The fears, the retreat, the desire for invisibility were all erected from the ground floor of unworthiness for love. Everything that happened stemmed from that faulty original conclusion that I couldn't be loved. That is the landing strip of my airport. That is the dock for my ship at sea.

That is why I called it quits for eighteen months.

CHAPTER 5

THE ESCAPE

We had a pet beagle which my wife and I would walk along the roads around our neighborhood. Being a beagle, she would pause constantly to take in the smells that we as humans could only guess were there. Sometimes if we were in a hurry, this slowed our pace considerably and I would get a little impatient with our progress, at which point I would apply my shoe to the part of her body under the tail. Now, don't sic the animal activists on me. I was quite gentle in my non-verbal instructions. It was just a little nudge on the south end going north to get the dog moving again.

This, in essence, is what happened near the end of my eighteen months of isolation. The nudge came in the form of a visit from my pastor.

Here I was, self-relegated to solitary confinement. There were no physical bars, no locks, no jailors, no prison walls, no barbed wire fences, yet I was as safely locked up as any prisoner in any federal penitentiary in the country. My emotions were my bars, locks, walls, and fences. I could physically leave any time I wanted, but I had reached the point where I didn't want to leave. I was content, unwilling to put up the fight necessary for freedom. Until my pastor showed up.

The exact words he said have long since escaped from my memory. But his message is chiseled in the marbled walls of my brain. In essence, he said that God would not put up with my situation forever, that there would come a time when He would write me off and give up on me.

Ouch! Those were tough words. They hit me like a Muhammed Ali uppercut. They also scared me. Whether he meant it to come across that way or not, that's the message I perceived. The problem was that it was an easy message to believe because it matched well with my understanding of God. Despite my one-time encounter with Hebrews 12:6, my estimation of God's character was not entirely accurate. Actually, it was just plain wrong. Mercy? What's that? Grace? That's something you said at the supper table. Peace? That's certainly nothing I had experienced. To me God was the great governor of the state of judgment. He was just looking for someone not living up to His standards so He could bring some kind of punishment down on them.

I had spent my entire life trying to measure up to people's expectations. In my estimation, I failed to attain those expectations which propelled me into emotional exile. And now here was my pastor effectively informing me that I was not meeting up to God's expectations either. What a downer. Again I say, ouch!

My pastor's words inflicted the first dent in the canopy of illusion I had erected around myself. Never again could I naively entertain the thought of spending the rest of my life in isolation without wondering if God would get fed up. My season of carefree living was about to end and reality began squeezing its way in. I now had to deal with a God whose tolerance level had been taxed to the limit.

How accurate was my pastor's assessment of God's character? We are taught in Psalms that His mercy endures forever. Romans 15:5 refers to Him as a God of patience. He is described many times as being slow to anger. Longsuffering is a fruit of the Spirit, and patience is a 1 Corinthians 13 characteristic of perfect love, which God is. Does there come a time when God reaches a point of exasperation? Does He ever give up on one of His children? After hearing my pastor's words, I wasn't sure, neither was I sure whether I wanted to find out.

The fact is that God wants His children to experience all that this life has to offer. He wants what's best for them, and that includes me. He wants me to live a full life.

Looking back, I don't think I was in danger of God giving up on me, even though at the time I wasn't convinced of that. Instead, I believe that God had used my afternoon studies of the Bible and verse memorization to build me up to a point where I was ready to move on out. He saw that. I sure didn't. And He used the words my pastor said to gently nudge me back into society.

We've all heard the saying that it's easier to steer a moving vehicle than one that is stationary. God just wanted to get me moving so He could guide me in the direction I needed to go. He had done the prep work for eighteen months, and it was now time to move on out.

The question was how! I had no idea. After over twelve months of counseling, after a year and a half of afternoon Bible study and memorization, after eighteen months of solitude with my thoughts, I was no closer to understanding myself than I was when my brain and stomach had their little conversation.

Here I was in a situation where I was afraid to go out because of what people might think of me, and now I was afraid to stay where I was because of what God might think of me.

I didn't want to disappoint God, something I thought I was seriously close to doing. But how could I avoid it? What could I do to circumvent the fear I always felt? How could I handle the physical manifestations of my fear that attacked me whenever I thought about heading back into society? What a predicament I was in!

I was really scared. I was afraid to go out. I was afraid to stay in. How could I possibly deal with this?

The words of my pastor clung to me like the words of the girl I met in Israel when she told me of my need to ask Jesus into my life at a specific point in time. Was he right? I had no reason to believe he wasn't. The thoughts butted against each other in my mind. I need to leave my prison, but I don't know how? It's time to live again, but it's too scary. God wants me to move on, but I am completely at a loss as to how to do it! I wore another path in my brain going back and forth. Should I finally try to overcome my fears and place myself in the unmerciful clutches of people again? Should I risk the potential hurt I might experience at the hands of human race? If so, how? I had no earthly idea what I needed to do to get it done.

After a season of reasoning with myself, I finally decided that I had to start moving. It was a compulsion, not a desire. To my way of thinking, God was forcing me to leave my sanctuary. I didn't want to, I had to because God had just about reached the end of His patience with me.

I had to figure out some way to escape from my prison. I had reduced my world to a small physical location. It had walls, windows, a floor, and a ceiling. I could see it with my eyes. I could touch it. My physical world was restricted to the upstairs rooms of my house. It was here where I felt safe. It was here where I felt secure. My goal, then, became to move beyond those four walls, but also take my safety and security with me. Emotional safety was the overriding concern. If I could somehow learn how to venture beyond the walls of my homemade prison while maintaining my sense of security, maybe I could return to society and thwart the impending judgment of God.

I did the only thing I knew. I ended up reenergizing my shield and taking my prison with me. And the only way I could figure on being successful in this endeavor was taking steps inch by inch, literally. To all of a sudden get in the car, drive to a store, walk in and buy something, and then drive home was completely out of the question. Just the thought of quitting my seclusion "cold turkey" like that pulverized any amount of resolution I had built up and sent me straight back to bed. My pilgrimage back to normalcy had to be done in small steps or it wouldn't be done at all. When I say small steps, I mean really, really small, but they were huge to me. I started by going downstairs one day when nobody was home, opening the front door from the kitchen and actually placing my foot on the porch. I spent a few seconds soaking in the atmosphere and then headed back to the comfort of my bedroom thoroughly satisfied with a full day's work well done.

The next day, I repeated the previous day's performance and built on it by taking a baby step away from the house. I was still on the porch and I could still physically touch the house, but I had established some space that detached me from structure that had become my sanctuary. Again pleased with this day's efforts I retreated back upstairs to rest from the exhaustive undertaking.

These small strides required several hours of mind-wrestling. It was no small matter to muster up the courage for even these seemingly meaningless steps. It required a significant amount of mental preparation and was really a day long activity by the time I actually performed the task.

Part of the reason these small steps were such an undertaking was because I knew the end result of my efforts. Eventually I would encounter the day when the next step would be contact with people out in the real world. Each small step onto the porch carried with it a recognition that what I feared the most would have to become a reality, that I was striving for something that scared the devil out of me. A simple step onto the front porch in and of itself was not greatly threatening. It was the foreknowledge of what would necessarily result from a multitude of these small steps that caused the hours of mental struggle each day. An inevitable date with people was always in the back of my mind.

You get the picture. It took several days to reach the steps that led from the porch to the sidewalk, another few days to descend to the sidewalk itself, and many more days of agonizing inch by agonizing inch to start seeing real progress. Each time I attained a new plateau I stood there to soak in the lack of danger in that place. I was trying to convince myself that I was going to be okay and that nothing could hurt me there. In reality I was carrying my emotional prison with me with each stride, persuading myself that the mental sheath I was generating was sufficient to dispel any danger that might arise. I was fortifying my defense against whatever peril presented itself. My shields were fully engaged.

The puniness of my efforts might seem a little laughable when looking back on it. I sure that someone who might have witnessed my efforts would have been puzzled or amused. But what do you think God thought about it? Since God is powerful enough to create and sustain all of the physical universe, surely He must have been bored to tears as I embarked on my miniscule efforts of escape. If anyone had the right to ridicule my feebleness, it was God. The Master of the universe, the One whose power stretches beyond what the most active of imaginations can conceive, the One who could destroy all that we see with a simple spoken word had every right to be condescending.

But I believe God was applauding each and every little baby step I was taking, just as we as parents are thrilled when our children stumble through their first few steps.

God is not as hard on us as we tend to believe He is because He possesses a complete knowledge of who we are. His understanding of our makeup is perfect. He knew how hard it was for me. He knew it wasn't easy leaving the comforts of prison. He knew it wasn't easy overcoming a past that had been ingrained into my very being. He knew how tough it was escaping the gravitational field of my planet of isolation. God is not harsh in dealing with us, understands our positions and applauds growth, no matter how small that growth is.

But I knew the time would soon arrive when I had to actually come into contact with those dreaded members of the human race. The inevitable reintegration into society was approaching. That thing I feared with every little step was getting closer. I could see the sun of normalcy starting to rise over the horizon and it was not very comforting. But I persisted in my efforts.

My next step was to actually get into my well rested car. Our farm sat about a quarter of a mile off the main road. I started by driving out our gravel lane and then backing back down the lane as there was not a good place to turn around where the lane intersected the road. This was followed by very short excursions down the street, turning around in a vacant driveway, and returning home. I usually took a right turn out of the driveway as a left turn directed me toward town. The right turn led me out into the farmland areas of Lancaster County. But soon I was able to turn left and venture into more populated areas, although still with no intention of stopping to get out. I even avoided stop signs and traffic lights whenever possible.

My halting baby steps gradually led to increasingly longer strides as I gained confidence that the emotional prison I traveled with was strong enough to handle the situation.

THE ISOLATION ROOM

Then it finally happened. I stopped for the first time in a year and a half to buy a drink at a convenience store. I drove by the store a number of days before I had the courage to stop. Did the people in the store know what a big undertaking this was for me? Did the cashier know who he was taking money from? I felt conspicuously on display, that everybody was looking at me as some kind of weirdo, like they all knew where I was coming from. I felt very exposed.

Little by little, I forced my way back into society, complete with my invisible prison walls. I wasn't doing anything different than what I had done before. I still didn't talk much. I still retreated into the background in social settings. I still mobilized my shields at the slightest contact with another person. I would get nauseated quite often, an attempt by my brain to force me back to where I was safe. Anxiety became a common experience. The threat of panic attacks edged their way into my life. I used my shield to deny their presence, just like I had done in the past.

After several months, I realized that I needed to find a job, which was especially upsetting. It was one thing to go out for an hour or so to do something knowing that if anxiety issues arose it was fairly easy to head back to the comfort and security of home. But to go to a job and be stuck there for eight or nine hours unable to conveniently leave if things got uncomfortable, that was an entirely different matter. How would I handle a situation where I became anxious sometime in the morning but was unable to get away until that afternoon? Could I survive that?

As it turns out, one of my uncles owned a machine shop in Lancaster and he needed someone to help him out in the office. He had to run the shop, but also do all the office paperwork himself and it was getting to be too much for him. So I went to work in my uncle's machine shop as his office manager. I answered the phone, reorganized his very unorganized filing system, made deliveries to local businesses who bought the parts his shop made, and generally did whatever needed to be done. It wasn't the most exciting of jobs, but it was just what I needed at the time, to work for a family member without the stress of employment in a company that didn't really care what kind of personal struggles you were going through. I worked alone most of the time and was able to control my anxieties fairly well with my fully activated shield. That issue of controlling my anxieties would figure prominently in the days to come.

That's how I forged my way back into society, by tiny increments of migration away from the safe and secure sanctuary of my room. So what did I do with my fears? Had I suddenly been delivered from worrying? Was I stress-free? How did I handle the physical manifestations of my fears, the nausea and sometimes chest pain? In fact if I heard about some disease and its symptoms, I was susceptible to feeling those symptoms. Imaginary pain was a constant companion. Was I now freed from all of that? Hardly!

In spite of a year of counseling I had not learned the first thing about how to handle my emotions. My modus operandi of the past was to suppress them, stuff them into the deep recesses of my being, to force them to the back burner of my mind. They were still not something I wanted to deal with. They were still annoying. They were still unwelcome. They still had nothing to offer me. Most importantly, I still didn't want to open myself up to others.

When I began crawling away from my upstairs shelter, the fears I had grown tired of fighting made their comeback. They returned to gnaw at me, trying to keep me in check, to prevent me from accomplishing the task of reentry into life. Naturally I returned to the tried and true methods of my past in dealing with them, and that was to deny their existence. Denial was how I had survived before, and it was how I would survive again. That's all I knew. Before my isolation I had reached the point of mental exhaustion and just couldn't keep up the fight. Here, it was almost like the eighteen months of rest had allowed me to get my second wind and I was now able to enlist the energy necessary protect myself.

In essence I was simply expanding the walls of my prison, or more accurately, I was taking my prison walls with me as I moved out. The four physical walls of my bedroom had been translated into four emotional walls that enveloped me as I moved out. They were walls of my own manufacturing for the purpose of not allowing what people did to affect me. I was basically returning to my roots.

When someone said something that should have been hurtful, I refused to feel hurt. I rejected feeling pain. After all, I was a Christian now and Christians aren't supposed to have negative feelings. The Christian life is one of victory, positivity, triumph. Negativity had no place in the life of a child of God, so I thought that by suppressing such thoughts, I was fulfilling the model of the Christian life.

By constructing my emotional bubble, I was handling things no differently than I had before my isolation except for one difference. I now had something else to help me. I had been given a survival tool called the Word of God, but it was a tool I didn't know how to use properly.

"Whack-A-Mole" has been a popular arcade game for decades. In this game the player has a whacker like a hammer in his hand and he stands in front of a number of holes. Each hole contains a mechanical mole. These moles poke their head out of the holes randomly for a very short time and the player is supposed to hit them in the head before they disappear back into their hole. The game requires quick reflexes to score and resembles pretty accurately the very real game I played with my fear.

"Whack-A-Fear" was my game. My whacker was the Word of God. As soon as fear exposed itself to me I quickly grabbed one of my whackers – 1 John 4:18 – and mentally quoted the words, "There is no fear in love, but perfect love casts out fear." Another good whacker was 2 Timothy 1:7 – "God has not given us a spirit of fear, but of power and of love and of a sound mind." My interpretation of these verses was this; no fear means no reality. If I was afraid, it was my job to deny it out of existence. I would recite the words very emphatically in my mind trying to shout down the fear. If I was alone, I'd sometimes say, even yell the words out loud. My goal was to drown out my fear with the verse I was quoting.

It was like when you have a towel that you've used to dry the flooded basement floor from a leaky wall after a heavy rain. Once the towel is saturated, you wring it out, squeezing and twisting it until you can't get any more water out. It takes some muscle and effort. Likewise, I was squeezing and twisting my mind trying to extract every morsel of fear I was feeling. It took significant mental effort until the fear was no longer discernable.

I wasn't using the Word of God to deal with the fear, I was using it to pound it back inside. My thinking was that since I was a Christian and I was loved, then fear was not supposed to be in my life. Therefore I had to make it not exist. I had to deny its presence because it does not belong in the life of a Christian. My rationale was that since the Bible said that there is no fear in love then when I felt fear it was something that did not really exist in my life. It wasn't supposed to be there, therefore it wasn't.

Instead of allowing God to use His Word to deal with

my fear, I felt like I had to do all the work myself. It was up to me to make it disappear because God already said that it didn't exist in the life of a Christian.

I was doing the exact same things to deal with my emotions that I had always done. I was rejecting them, denying their existence, whacking them back when they got in the way, generally just replicating what I had done my entire life. Nothing had changed.

If I had to summarize what I was looking for when I holed myself up for that year and a half, my primary goal was to find a place of safety where I didn't feel threatened. I longed for a sanctuary. I was desperate for security. I yearned for peace. I craved for a refuge from the battles I had fought throughout my entire life. I wanted somewhere to relax my mind and just be myself. I needed rest and that's what I had for eighteen months.

As I returned to the land of the living, facilitated by my pastor and a God who had just about had enough, my goal remained unchanged. My need for safety was just as relevant. The issues I had before were still unresolved. I still needed security, peace, sanctuary. But somehow I had to achieve these things outside of the friendly confines of my bedroom. I no longer had four physical walls surrounding me to keep me safe, so I had to create replacements. I strived to build my own emotional walls that were just as solid as the physical ones I was leaving.

Controlling my anxieties would be a recurring issue. Any time I encountered a situation that could be construed as threatening in some way, the red on my anxiety thermometer rose. And those situations were many.

I was always afraid of "losing it" when I felt like I was not in control. Losing it meant having some kind of panic attack. This happened in situations that seemed beyond my ability to control, essentially when I perceived that some other entity was calling the shots and there was no escape route to get away from what was causing the anxiety. I feared being locked into a situation.

If I was driving in stop and go traffic and came on a red light my anxiety level rose. I had lost control of the situation. That red light was now my master. If I had a panic attack, my only escape was to back up and drive the wrong way on the street. If another car came up to my rear effectively blocking me in, then even that possibility was taken away. I had nowhere to go if my anxiety increased too much. When the light turned green I once again sensed a measure of control.

Eating at a restaurant was another issue of control. I wasn't worried about what I was going to eat. The problem of where we would be seated consumed my thoughts much more than what food I was going to order. The hostess leading us was in control, making my decision for me. I dreaded being seated somewhere in the middle of the room where I would have to pass by a number of people in the event of a panic attack. I much preferred a place along the wall, most preferable near a door or the bathrooms. Even the "buzzer will sound" door brought a sense of comfort because at least I could get away if I needed to, albeit with much fanfare. When we were seated, I took inventory of the surroundings, mapping out my escape routes. I liked having my back to the wall, able to see everything that was going on. This somehow gave me a perception of control that I didn't have if I couldn't see the business being conducted behind my back.

Walking into a major department store was unsettling as well. The farther into the bowels of this massive room I had to go, the greater the sense of uneasiness because the door of escape was retreating behind me. My escape routes became more problematic the farther toward the middle I had to go. The location of what I was there to buy was the entity in control. And of course, waiting in the checkout line evoked the same kind of anxieties I felt in stop and go traffic. The speed of the cashier and the number of people in the checkout lane were the issues then.

If I had to travel with a group of people, I always offered to drive. It just gave me a sense of being more in control of my circumstances. If I was riding then my sense of commanding my own destiny was greatly diminished. If I was able to sit by the door it was easier, although I don't know what I thought I was going to do at sixty miles an hour.

No matter what course of events I encountered, two things were constant. I wanted to be in control, and I wanted to have a means of escape should the need arise. The red light was in control in city traffic. The person seating us at the restaurant was in control. The positioning of what I had to buy in the department store controlled where I had to go. The cashier and the people in front of me controlled how long it took me to get through the line. The person driving the vehicle on the trip was the master.

In each of these and myriads of other circumstances, I was always searching out an avenue of escape, the nearest door, the nearest restroom, the quickest way to get away from the people around me, the shortest route to solitude. If I discovered a fairly easy way to vanish from my situation then my anxiety level lowered in correspondence to the ease of escape. If no easy escape presented itself then my anxiety level remained high until the activity I was engaged in was done.

I wanted to be in control. Escape was one of the ways I felt like I could remain master of my circumstances.

The thing about all of this is that I never really "lost it" to the extent that I had to radically run from a situation. I was afraid that I might have to escape, but the need to actually escape never materialized. One of the things my pastor said when he spoke to me was in the form of a rhetorical statement. He said, "I bet you die a thousand deaths." He meant that I worried about things that never happened. If worries could have been counted, my number would have been astronomical. I worried so much about what could happen that I never enjoyed the experiences I was actually having.

Worry is a thief. It steals any joy we might feel from the life that God has given to us. I had to learn that I don't have to be in control when I am held in the hand of God. He is in control of everything I will encounter, past, present, and especially future. Why worry about something that God has already made provision for? Worry is the down payment we unnecessarily pay for a purchase that God has already made. These are easy things to write down in a paragraph, but to put them into practice is quite a task. It's an endeavor of a lifetime.

I mentioned that during this eighteen month hiatus from life, I spent a lot of time watching television. One of the programs that intrigued me was the church service from Thomas Road Baptist Church with Dr. Jerry Falwell called The Old Time Gospel Hour. He kept talking about a college he had just started a few years earlier in Lynchburg, VA. I wondered if I would ever be able to go there. It seemed like such a great place to be.

When I got back to working and doing somewhat normal activity, the possibility of attending what was then Liberty Baptist College began to formulate in my mind. The school had a major in television production, and because I had watched so much TV as I was growing up, the thought of actually being a part of producing TV programs sounded good to me. So in January of 1977, at the age of 23, I enrolled in Liberty Baptist College, (later to become Liberty University) and majored in television production.

The fact that I was able to do this amazes me to this day. God was truly working in my life

CHAPTER 6

THE MOVE

It's about as close to an out-of-body experience as I'll ever have. On a cold January day, my parents and I drove across the James River into downtown Lynchburg, Virginia, and I got the first look at my new home. The centerpiece of the skyline was the 20 story bank building two streets up from the river. A block farther featured the seventeen story Allied Arts building, and that's about all that was impressive about Lynchburg's downtown. The rest was rather drab to be honest. Lots of dark red brick buildings that reminded me of warehouses adorned the riverbank, none of them over a couple of stories tall. The lack of excitement in the skyline didn't help calm my nerves.

I was a year and a half removed from re-entry into society and the bridge over the river might as easily have been a bridge to Mars as I surveyed my new home city, feeling like I was approaching some planet in a galaxy far, far away.

Considering my past experiences away from home, the week in Colorado, the weekend visit to a college in Ohio, I can be excused for feeling some apprehension on that January day. Here I was, crossing two bridges, a physical bridge across a river, and an emotional bridge spanning the chasm between an insecure past and an unknown future. Here I was entering a city I had never been to knowing that in a few short hours my parents would leave to go back to Pennsylvania and I would be left on my own, not just for a weekend visit, but for the next four years. What was I thinking?

THE ISOLATION ROOM

Of course, my shield was in high gear. My fear-whacker was just a blur as it whacked down fear after fear after fear. We all know that fear should not be in the life of a Christian who is trusting God, right?

When I started at what was then Liberty Baptist College, there was no campus. It had been founded just six years earlier by Dr. Jerry Falwell. Little did I know the prominent role, the incredible influence he would have on my future life. The college rented various buildings around the city as dorms. Classes were held in an old high school that the city had abandoned and was on the verge of demolishing to make room for a new one. Old rundown green and white school buses were familiar sights on the roads of Lynchburg as they transported students between these various dorms and the classroom building.

One dorm was Treasure Island, an old summer youth camp in the middle of the James River a couple of miles north of downtown. A long winding road barely wide enough for two cars to pass, let alone two buses, led from Rivermont Avenue down the river's embankment to a bridge that spanned the James River from the southern banks to the island. This so-called bridge would test your faith. To get on or off the island, the bus stopped at one end of the bridge and everyone except the driver had to get off. The empty bus then crossed the 150 foot bridge followed by the passengers who hoofed it over the rickety span and then reentered the bus to be transported to their destination. They were afraid if the bus crossed the bridge with a full load...well, buses don't float.

There was the "hotel" located downtown on the corner of Church and Eighth Streets. From the outside it looked like just another one of those drab, red brick buildings I saw while crossing over the James River. Inside was different. We called it the hotel because that's what it was

71

for many years, "The Virginian," a six story structure used by travelers to the city. It was unique because it had a grand lobby, a second floor which overlooked the lobby, the two floors linked together by a majestic marble staircase, narrow at the top and widening out into a semi-circle as it reached the lobby, ala Cinderella's Ball. The elevator was quite capable of making it to the first floor, but the girls often opted to get off on floor two so they could take advantage of the splendor of the marble staircase as they presented themselves to their dates for the evening. About half of the grand lobby had been transformed into a cafeteria. It was quite a high class adventure to live there while attending a college with no campus.

Dorm assignments were handed out in this lobby and I was understandably anxious entering this statuesque edifice on that January afternoon. I had never lived anywhere but near my hometown of Lancaster, PA, yet here I was about a six hour car ride from anything I could call comfortable, wondering if I could make it after all I had experienced. My nerves were making a nuisance of themselves.

At this point, I knew nothing about the "campus" spread out all over the town as I walked up to the table to learn where I would call home that first semester. The girl handed me my dorm assignment and I learned that I was staying at the Ramada Inn. At first I thought "Ramada Inn" might just be an affectionate nickname for one of the dorm buildings around Lynchburg. Not so. It was actually the Ramada Inn located about ten blocks from where I was standing. The college had rented a good portion of the hotel as a men's dorm, complete with an outdoor pool. So far, so good.

The one downside was that no meals were served at the Ramada Inn. To eat, I had to walk to the cafeteria that was in the old hotel in which I was standing at that moment. It was a ten block trek through the downtown streets and it didn't matter what the weather was like. If I wanted to eat, I had to walk.

But even this scenario had an upside because conveniently situated at the halfway point of the ten block walk was a Hardee's. There were many times when I had every intention of eating in the cafeteria to consume food I had already paid for. However, the Hardee's hamburger smell drifting out to the street from their kitchen was sometimes just too tempting. Pitting the cafeteria food against a Hardee's hamburger and fries was not a fair fight.

But beyond that, stopping at Hardee's also freed me from the social pressures of the cafeteria. I didn't have to wonder if there was a seat safe enough for me. Every time I entered the cafeteria, I quickly surveyed the territory. Tables with girls were completely off limits. Not a chance I'd sit with them. I was looking for "safe" people. These were the kids that I felt less threatened by. Perhaps they were members of some of my classes, or other students in my television production major. If they were sitting at a table with an empty chair, I'd hurry through the line hoping to get there before someone else grabbed the seat. If there were no opportunities of that kind available, I'd gravitate toward the emptiest table I could find, hoping that one of my "safe" people would arrive and sit by me so I wouldn't have to eat alone. I didn't like eating alone, but it was preferable to forcing myself into an uncomfortable situation.

Hardee's presented a nice reprieve a number of times from the social anxieties of the cafeteria.

We pulled into the hotel parking lot. The room I was assigned to was around the back on the second floor. These were the kind of rooms that you entered from the outside and the walkway overlooked the James River, although foliage obliterated most of the view.

We began unpacking the car, and what a job that was. If you remember the movie E.T. there was a scene where the mother opens the closet door as if looking for something. The camera pans away from her and across to a mountain of toy animals. In the middle was the face, and only the face of the alien, surrounded by all varieties of stuffed animals. Lions, and tigers, and bears, oh my!

That's pretty much what I looked like in the back seat of my parents' car for the six hour drive to college. I tried to bring as much of home as would fit and still leave a place for me to sit. The trunk was stuffed, I was straitjacketed between the door and my cherished possessions. I think the rearview mirror was still at least partially useful to my dad, but I'm not sure.

As we entered the room I soon realized that a lot of the things I brought were going back to Pennsylvania. It was a normal sized room for hotel use, but it shrunk significantly when filled with a bunk bed, another twin bed, and three dressers, one for each of the guys who would call it home for the semester. Once my stuff was inside, it was clear that all of it couldn't stay. I was one of three in the room and if I kept everything I had brought, some of it would have ended up in the river, tossed there by disgruntled roommates.

Half of what I brought had to go back with my parents. The problem was deciding what I would have to live without. Of course, the essentials stayed, such as clothes, toiletries and school necessities. But I had also brought a lot of things that were more emotional in nature. I wanted to bring to college as much home security as I could, to hang onto as much of home as I possibly could. The question was, then, how to discern between what stayed and what went back to Pennsylvania?

I attacked the task with ferocity, like I had a time limit for finishing the assignment. You'd think that I would have agonized over each piece of sentimentality. It should have been extremely difficult to part with all the things I had to send back. The truth is, it didn't take long at all. I went right to work creating two piles, the "staying" pile, and the "leaving" pile. I grabbed an object and almost immediately it was flying through the air toward one of the two piles. My parents had to dodge and duck to keep from being hit. I gave as much thought to my undertaking as a mother does while separating the whites from the colors for a load of wash. I wasn't allowing myself to think too long about any of the objects. I was making my decisions faster than Watson, the IBM computer.

The reason was that I couldn't afford to allow myself to feel anything in regard to what I was sending back. If my hands held something that I was emotionally attached to for too long, I was afraid I wouldn't be able to part with it, sensing the loss of security associated with each object. I was afraid that if I experienced such loss too many times, I might just throw myself into the "leaving" pile and head home. The speed at which I made my decisions was a defense mechanism against feeling too much. So I picked up an object, and a second later it was airborne toward one of the two piles. Once the task was completed, we loaded the "leaving" pile into the trunk. Out of sight, out of mind.

The next day my parents left to go back home. I watched in silent disbelief as their car faded into the distance, heading for the expressway and a six hour drive north. What was I doing? Was I really and truly moving out of the house? Was I actually embarking on a life of my own? Was this the transition time to beat all other transition times? Standing there on the sidewalk in front of the hotel, it hit me that I was actually doing it. I was beginning to live on my own, and it scared the crap out of me. Of course, I never admitted it at the time. As their car turned the last corner out of sight, I turned to face a new reality, having no earthly idea what experiences lay ahead of me.

Did I feel alone? You bet! I was a freshman, a mid-year freshman at that, and there weren't many of us starting in January. My roommates were upper classmen, which meant that I arrived on "campus" about a week before they did.

That first week, Lynchburg was hit with an ice storm that decimated all the freshman orientation activities that had been scheduled. Because the new freshman were scattered around four different dorm locations around the city, and because the buses were unable to travel, I really never met very many people until the returning students showed up the next weekend and classes started.

Due to the lack of parking, freshmen were not allowed to have their own cars, so I left mine in Pennsylvania. But shortly after school began I learned that since I was 23 years old, I was exempt from that rule. Boy was that great news. I could have my car, but how was I to get it to Lynchburg?

It turns out that one of my roommates was on the wrestling team, and just a few weeks into the semester, they had a meet in Harrisburg, Pennsylvania, about a forty minute drive from my house. I hitched a ride on the team bus, my dad picked me up and I drove my car back to Lynchburg.

I was excited by this turn of events for two reasons. First, I was no longer dependent on sometimes undependable green and white school buses. It gave me more mobility, and of course, friends because I had a car. Second, and more importantly, my car was my escape mechanism should I need one. I was still formulating my exit strategies in vulnerable situations. Riding those old buses between the various sites around the city was somewhat threatening because of the control issue. If I wasn't at the wheel, I wasn't in control. When we left one location, my anxiety level increased. When we arrived at the next location, I calmed down. During the trip there was no dignified way to escape from the loaded bus peddling its way down the expressway. Now that I had my car it gave me more control over my life. I could hop into my car and speed away from whatever was threatening me. If things got too bad I could keep going until I reached the farm. My car was my escape pod. Before then, it would have been a long walk back to Pennsylvania. Before my car I was really quite stranded in my new city. I now had an avenue of retreat should it be necessary.

My car was a Plymouth Duster, gold with a black hood and trim. When I became a Christian I did a custom paint job on it. On the black hood I stenciled all the words to John 3:16 with gold paint. On the gold trunk the stenciling was done in black, this time it was all of John 14:6. Why? I had an urging from deep within to do something special, something to get me noticed. I always felt like I wasn't good enough just as I was, like I had to perform some fantastic feat to gain acceptance. Because I was such a disaster in one on one situations, I had to do things to make myself satisfactory to people. I felt like I had to be the best athlete on the team, or the smartest kid in the class, or the hero who saved someone from a burning building. The problem was that I didn't have the confidence in myself to actually do those things, so most of my extraordinary exploits were done only in my mind. Normally pretend friends and proxy experiences are joys relegated to children, not adults. But I maintained a steady diet of pretenses in my own mind, all with the goal of making myself adequate to engage with people. These were imaginary fronts that I mentally propped myself up with when dealing with people. They gave me a false sense of importance which gave me the courage to engage in human interaction, at least on the surface. Without these fronts I was completely intimidated and nervousness permeated me inside. I'm not sure if these fronts were apparent to the people around me, but they were absolutely vital for my own sense of significance.

This need for significance continued after I became a Christian. I felt like in order to be pleasing to God I had to do something of a grand nature for Him to accept me. I wasn't good enough just being the person I was. I needed to do something more notable. This was not a question of salvation, but of having to do more to gain God's approval. I just couldn't believe that God would love and accept me for who I was without anything else. Unconditional love was a completely foreign concept. It wasn't possible. God could not just love me as I was. I had to do things to somehow earn that love. So I painted my car with John 3:16 and John 14:6 to prove to God that I was worthy of His acceptance. My heart was in the right place by wanting to spread His Word, even if my actions were a bit out there.

I remember one time that first year I was standing at a window in our classroom building with two other guys overlooking the parking lot. They commented about my car, of course not knowing that the owner was standing next to them, expressing that while they saw nothing wrong with identifying oneself as a Christian on their car, they thought the stenciling on mine was a bit much. That's all the wording they used, just "a bit much." They didn't say it was stupid or idiotic or insanity or any other such hurtful words. Even though their wording was not severe, and nothing they said could be construed as mean-spirited, it felt like a Mohammed Ali right cross knocking me to the canvas. Although I never let on that they were talking about my car, their words actually shamed me. I actually felt ashamed of my car from that point on, highlighting how vulnerable I was to the opinions of others. It was at that moment that I determined to get a new car. I loved the black and gold color scheme and sleek design of my car, but the opinions of two guys who I didn't even really know made me ashamed of what I had done to it. The following summer my dad found a plain white car that had been in a flood up to the floorboard. He bought it for half price and I was quite relieved to no longer be seen in that embarrassing black and gold car that I had mistreated. Again, other people had tremendous influence over how I thought or felt about things.

Every time I think back on these days I am amazed and astounded that I survived. I was so unsure, fearful, so lacking in the ordinary tools for daily living. I can only point to the grace of God and His plan for my life as He instilled the strength I needed as I encountered the challenges of each day.

The four years I spent in college were somewhat uneventful as far as my emotional state was concerned. There were no major crises but that doesn't mean that the significance of what I was doing was lost on me. The only reason there was no major crisis was because I was pretty successful at keeping everything under control. But the loneliness remained even though I was almost constantly in the midst of people.

I continued avoiding as energetically as possible every opportunity for a social life. I immersed myself in my studies many times using that as the excuse I needed to not participate in social activities. I was usually too busy studying or I was working on a class project. I had to do all my schoolwork to the best of my ability leaving nothing undone, an admirable trait on the surface, but my motivation was avoidance of anything that would undermine my security. My inert studies were a preferable alternative to perilous social interaction.

Every time there was an event that involved television, I sprinted to volunteer to work it, which gave me a lot of experience in my career field, but also served to provide my excuse to avoid social contact. That's an issue I would finally resolve a few years after I graduated.

My fears were not too severe when in a group situation such as a class. It was in between classes, walking the hallways and sidewalks where I was uncomfortable. It was in the few minutes before a class would start, when everyone around me was carrying on a conversation with somebody and I was standing there wishing I was talking to someone myself, but unwilling to take the initiative to speak the first word. Again, I really had precious little to actually talk about unless it involved what was happening around us at the time such as homework or how boring a class was. Personal glimpses of my life were off limits, not because I didn't want to divulge anything, but because I didn't have anything to divulge. I still had no real understanding of who I was and I'm not sure how willing I would have been to reveal those details if the opportunity ever came up.

College life was nothing more than a reliving of my teen years. I still wished I had the courage to be like the other guys and interact with the girls, but the fears of my teens continued unabated into my early twenties. Very little progress was seen in this area.

Physically I was able to cope and that's about it. My stomach issues continued. The fear of panic when in situations beyond my control remained. I would sometimes sit through class, my right hand taking notes on top of the desk and my left hand strategically placed on my stomach trying to make it feel better. I don't know if others noticed this because I did my best to keep it clandestine. Amazingly, as the end of class neared, my stomach would start feeling better. As long as I was in the middle of class, the clock on the wall was in control and there was nothing I could do to make it go faster. At the end of class I could get up and be in control again.

As if stomach discomfort wasn't enough, another physical manifestation began to appear as well – headaches – and they were doozies. I hated waking up with one because I knew that if I had a headache when I woke up it would stay with me all day and make it miserable. Eating became problematic on these days and classroom concentration was quite difficult. I'm not sure if they were migraines, but if they weren't, they were pretty close.

The first thing I did when I woke up with one of these was take a couple of aspirins. Depending on the severity two more pills went down the hatch about an hour later and two more an hour or two after that. This was a daylong affair. They didn't take the headache away, they just took the edge off a little. These pills became kind of like comfort food for me on my headache days. As soon as I took one set of two I'd count the minutes until it was time for the next dose. Occasionally four pills at a time would make their way into my bloodstream. I was just trying to lessen the severity of the pain to a tolerable level. Twelve to twenty pills later I'd lay my head on my pillow with great relief because I knew I would feel better in the morning. Very rarely did I have these headaches two days in a row. When I woke up on a headache day I couldn't wait until nighttime when I could go to sleep and experience relief knowing that tomorrow would be better.

As I said, I avoided the social life as much as possible by immersing myself in my studies and volunteering for every television event there was. The result was a final GPA of 3.922, a number my dad really liked.

A few weeks before graduation I got a job at the local ABC affiliate as a production assistant, a fancy name for the person who does whatever needs doing. I operated a studio camera for the newscasts for eight months, a part-time job, followed by a full-time position as the film director. No, I didn't direct any movies. I just handled all the commercials, shows, and movies that aired on film instead of videotape. My favorite part of the year and a half was putting the commercial breaks into the Star Trek episodes that the station aired. It was awesome to watch my favorite show and get paid for it.

The final three years at the station was spent in the newsroom as a news photographer. I covered the White House twice when local groups were getting awards from President Reagan. I battled through the summer heat covering the twentieth anniversary of the Martin Luther King march on Washington. I shot video of myriads of stories from trials, to crimes, to fires, to elections, to features. But after a few years of news gathering in Lynchburg, Virginia, the stories tended to repeat themselves every year and I began to get bored. How many different ways can you shoot a city council meeting?

It was at this time that the television ministry of Jerry Falwell approached me and offered me the job of traveling with Jerry Falwell wherever he went during the week. I was then to produce a segment on his exploits for a show that aired live on Sunday nights on WTBS in Atlanta. This was during the height of the "Moral Majority" days and it was quite an inviting offer, which I accepted.

A year later I married and my wife and I raised three children together. My job evolved after a few years into editing the Thomas Road Baptist Church Sunday morning service and transforming that into "The Old-Time Gospel Hour" syndicated television show that aired on hundreds of stations around the country.

While there were a few emotional crises during these years, most of the time God was just steadily working in my life to free me from the leftover shackles of my self-imposed prison. Slow but sure growth marked my life as God matured me away from my eighteen months of isolation.

But one event impacted me like no other, leading me to an understanding of God like I had never had before.

CHAPTER 7

THE TURNING POINT

We were all gathered in a room behind the stage of Thomas Road Baptist Church. The date was Tuesday, May 15, 2007. It was almost time for our weekly meeting with Dr. Jerry Falwell. As line producer and editor of "The Old-Time Gospel Hour," I was there with others of the television department, as well as some members of the management team of the ministry. It was about 10:45. The meeting was scheduled for 11:00.

Dr. Falwell was very busy as you might imagine, but he was also very punctual. If he was going to be late for a meeting, either he or his secretary would call someone to tell them he was running late.

11:00 came and 11:00 went – no Jerry.

At 11:10, still no Jerry...or phone call. This was unusual. Some folks in the room started making calls of their own trying to track down our wayward pastor.

At 11:20, the Chief Operating Officer of the ministry, an attendee of our meeting, informed us that the meeting was canceled, but offered no explanation.

Within the hour, a ministry-wide staff meeting was announced for 2:00 that afternoon.

We started fearing the worst.

At 2:00, our fears were confirmed. Dr. Jerry Falwell had died.

To say that Dr. Falwell's passing impacted everyone in the ministry would be to grossly understate the obvious. He had begun Thomas Road Baptist Church in 1956 with just thirty-five charter members. He pioneered a television ministry a year later, which eventually mushroomed into an international network of stations that aired the church's Sunday morning services. In 1967 he launched a K-12 Christian day school. Then in 1971 he founded Liberty Baptist College with only 154 students. That school is now Liberty University which attracts students from all over the world through its residential and online programs. His activities in the political arena, especially during the 1970's and 1980's are well documented. He and others established the Moral Majority, which propelled Ronald Reagan into the presidency. Dr. Jerry Falwell's influence in our country, as well as his influence in the lives of everyone inside the ministry, can hardly be overstated.

However, the Jerry Falwell portrayed in the media and by his enemies was not at all the Jerry Falwell that I knew. While a lot of people considered him their enemy, in his mind he had no enemies, just people who had not yet learned about a personal God who loved them and wanted to have a relationship with them. And it was this Jerry that I came to love and appreciate. I just didn't understand how much until after he died.

Jerry did not act like the big shot he could have been. There were no limos roaming the streets of Lynchburg carting him from place to place. He drove a Chevy Suburban SUV – he drove it himself, he refused to be chauffeured. He'd often come into the studio carrying the McDonald's bag he'd just picked up at the drive-thru.

One afternoon, we were taping some segments for the show, finishing near the end of the day. When we were done, he informed us that his car was in the garage and asked if he could hitch a ride home. I was leaving for the day anyway and so I gave him a ride home just like I would have for any of my co-workers.

Jerry knew that under God, everyone was equal. As

leader of the ministry, of course, he was responsible for making the decisions and setting the direction the organization would go. And we were responsible to carry those decisions out. But you always got the sense from him that you were just as important as he was. He valued you as a person and as a significant contributor to the ministry, no matter what your job was. Whether you were a custodian or a dean, you were of equal value because he knew that was how God viewed people. He esteemed each and every person as an individual.

Jerry had the kind of personality that was easy to get close to. He was your friend from the moment he met you. He never talked down to you. He always treated you as an equal. He could take a joke as easily as dish one out, and he dished out a lot.

Nearly everyone had a story to tell about "Jerry" as he was fond of being called. He cherished sneaking up on students in his Suburban and unleashing his "souped up" horn on them. You could hear it a quarter of a mile away. He loved watching a big, strapping football player jump like a child at the blare of his horn. They'd turn around and look at him in the driver's seat just laughing his head off.

Once I was in my car, parked and waiting for someone or something, I can't remember which. I was just relaxing there listening to the radio, unaware that Jerry was approaching me from the rear. Suddenly, I felt a jolt. Jerry had actually nudged my car with his Suburban. I turned around and saw him with the biggest grin. No, I didn't report an accident. It was no accident.

If you were a young, athletic type of guy meeting Jerry for the first time, you would do well to cover up. He'd either shake your hand or playfully punch you in the stomach. You never knew which was coming. Pity the guy he punched once who a few days earlier had cracked a couple of ribs.

My favorite experience involving Jerry took place on Monday, September 2, 1985, shortly after I began working for the ministry. It was Labor Day and Jerry flew to Dallas to speak at an anti-pornography rally. They were attempting to get Seven Eleven to remove porn magazines from the checkout lines because they were in full view of children. I went along as a videographer to document his appearance there, and our department secretary, who had never flown with Jerry to an event, came along to help me with the equipment. These were the days when a videographer had to carry a camera, tripod, recorder, and utility bag with extra batteries tapes, lights, and cords, and I needed someone to help carry this 100 pounds of equipment around Dallas. Everything went smoothly and we were on the flight back to Lynchburg when I noticed something strange happening.

There were nine people on the eight-seat ministry-owned jet. The ninth person had to sit on the toilet in the back. The secretary and I were perched on a two-person bench in the front right behind the pilots, facing the door. I noticed that one of the guys in the first row of seats was buckling his seat belt. We were a long way from landing and the pilot had not notified us of any air turbulence or storms up ahead, although we did get a distant view of Hurricane Helen that was molesting the Gulf Coast at the time. I asked the guy what was going on and he said that he wasn't totally sure, but he suggested that we might want to buckle up as well. We obliged and I secured the camera on my lap.

A few seconds later the mystery was revealed. The jet banked sharply to the left and nosedived. We began what felt like a free fall toward the surface. It reminded me of that first hill on a roller coaster that I've always hated. After we leveled off I looked at the readout in the cabin that reported the speed and altitude of the plane. We had dropped a mile in about ten seconds. Thirty seconds later, we did it a second time.

Jerry had gotten wind of the fact that this was our secretary's first trip on the ministry jet and so he just had to initiate the rookie. He had phoned up to the pilot and requested the aerial maneuvers. I wonder about the conversation the air traffic controllers were having with our pilot.

I looked back at Jerry after the second nosedive. He was grinning impishly from ear to ear, and assuring us that we were done playing roller coaster with the jet. He was obviously having a great time. The same could not be said of our secretary. She had been reading a magazine prior to the aerial hi-jinx. Afterward she was still trying to read, but with hands shaking like they were on a jackhammer. Jerry loved having fun with people.

The students of the university loved him as well, and he loved them. He enjoyed walking around campus and interacting with them. He was a common sight at athletic contests. At one of our basketball games, the students were chanting, "Jerry, Jerry, Jerry," beckoning him to come across to their section on the other side of the arena. Of course, he knew that they were up to something. Even so, at halftime, he obediently walked across the arena, took off his suit coat, and body-surfed all the way to the top of the 8,000 seat arena and back down again. We were all praying that the students wouldn't drop him. He was, after all, over sixty years old and not exactly at his optimum weight, but he'd do anything for the kids. He always considered himself to be a youth pastor. He loved young people.

I am spending this time describing the kind of person Jerry Falwell was because it relates to a crisis in my life that brought me to an understanding of our Heavenly Father that I had never known before. Quite often over the years I would hear people talk about Dr. Falwell in relational terms. I would hear comments like, "He was just like a brother to me." Others would say, "He's just like the father I never had." Such was the effect he had on people. He was just so easy to get close to.

I have often wondered about the kind of personality Jesus had. There's a rich man sitting at a table, collecting taxes. Jesus walks by and says, "Follow Me." That's it! No explanations, no negotiations, no promises. Just those two words. This man, Matthew, abruptly leaves his prosperity to follow someone who didn't have a home and no apparent means of income.

Jesus walks by the Sea of Galilee. There are two fishermen washing their nets on the shore. Jesus again says to them, "Follow Me, and I will make you fishers of men." They abruptly leave their father and the only occupation they know to pursue a future that was uncertain at best.

What kind of magnetism did Jesus have that seemingly level-headed people would follow him, not having the foggiest idea of where they were going? What kind of charisma, what kind of allure did Jesus have that drew people away from everything they knew to wander the countryside? The attraction emanating from Jesus must have been amazing.

Jerry Falwell had at least a portion of this same kind of aura. The minute he walked into the room, you were his best friend. You were drawn to him. It was as if it was just the two of you in the room, and there were twenty others in the same room thinking the same thing.

My duties with the television ministry, specifically with the "Old Time Gospel Hour" program included attending meetings with him on nearly a weekly basis. So I was exposed to his engaging, easy to get to know personality quite often. The fact that he entrusted his television show to me was also of great consequence. His trust in my work was very significant to me. I was about to find out just how significant it was.

I don't mean to complain, but I think God could have chosen a better time to take Jerry home. Another week or two later would have been nice because the following Saturday was Commencement for Liberty University. Twenty thousand people would show up on the campus to watch their friends and family members graduate. There wasn't a vacant hotel room within fifty miles of Lynchburg. Of course, Jerry's funeral would bring in a few thousand more visitors who had nowhere to stay, so the decision was made to hold the funeral the following Tuesday to give the graduation crowd time to clear out and make room for the next group.

For those of us working in the television area there was no time to think. Overnight the parking lot of the church sprouted what was known at the time as the state flower of West Virginia. Network satellite trucks took root beaming the story of Jerry's life and death to the world. Media requests for historical footage had to be fulfilled. Every event surrounding Jerry's death had to be documented and placed in historical archives. His body was displayed in the atrium of the DeMoss Learning Center building to give students a chance to pay their last respects, followed by a move by horse-drawn carriage to the church sanctuary for church members and townspeople to do the same. All of this was videoed for archival.

On top of that the Commencement exercises of Liberty University were always televised live and preparations had to be made for that broadcast. Former Speaker of the House, Newt Gingrich, was the commencement speaker that year which brought its own media attention down on us. It was determined that the funeral would also be broadcast live and those plans had to be solidified. Our cameras documented each and every event of that week making the few of us on the television staff extremely busy.

Personally, I was a little disappointed at my inability to properly mourn. It may have been that the hectic activity during that time was a factor, but I don't think it was the main reason.

Sitting in that 2:00 staff meeting announcing his death, I wanted to cry, but the tears just wouldn't come. I knew they should, but they just weren't there – just a small whimper.

Another whimper when my family passed the casket in the church. Again, not the kind of response I was expecting or wanting.

I was selected to be the photographer at the family's private graveside service. As the casket was lowered into the ground, another whimper.

Over the years, I had seen much improvement in the area of letting my emotions see the light of day, if not outwardly, at least enough to acknowledge their existence to myself. Now, in the midst of a time of what should have been a decent sized emotional demonstration, there was next to nothing.

The routine of life returned, and so did something else.

Over the course of a few weeks, anxiety began making a comeback. I'd wake up in the morning anxious about going to work. I'd leave work at the end of the day anxious about going home. The intensity of anxiety increased steadily as the days passed.

I had experienced this a few times over the years, and one of the lessons I learned was to always take that first step. One time, I was working as a news photographer at the local ABC affiliate. I was to leave with a reporter to shoot a story in the next few minutes. I was sitting in the editing room frozen to my chair, scared to the gills. Not sure why I was scared, I just was. There was no way I could rise from my seat to leave for that story.

When the reporter turned the corner asking if I was ready to go, what was I going to do? Would I go, or would I remain riveted to my seat?

Because of what I had learned, I took the first step. It was not easy in the least. Amazingly, by the time I took the second step, my anxiety level had decreased by at least eighty percent. The third step brought another reduction and I was able to do the story with very little trouble.

Fear and anxiety are harsh taskmasters who desire to keep us in check. They don't care about us as persons. They are prison guards whose job is to keep us where we are.

Fear and anxiety are shouters. There is nothing subtle about their methods. They yell in our ears that you can't do this. You aren't able. You aren't worthy. You don't measure up. They want to keep us from moving forward.

Some fears are normal. I am scared of heights. I don't bungee jump. I don't climb up vertical cliffs. I have trouble with ladders after about five rungs. This is not the kind of fear I am referring to here.

Fears that keep us from moving out, doing activities that are just normal for most people, these are the ones that are worthy of battling.

When I took that first step from my chair that day, I was responding to my fear with a big, resounding, "NO!!! You will not dictate to me what I am doing! You will not be my master!" It's okay to get mad at these kinds of fears. They are your enemy.

I almost give these kinds of fears a sense of personhood,

because when it is all traced back, we end up at sin and Satan. Fear did not exist until Satan enticed Adam and Eve to sin. In fact, the very first recorded emotion our original parents experienced was fear, (Genesis 3:10). Satan is our enemy. Sin is our enemy. Fear is our enemy. It's okay to treat them as enemies.

Getting back to after the funeral, my anxiety level increased as the days went by, but I kept exercising my right to take that first step.

Until one morning. I woke up cemented to my bed. I was shaking involuntarily and scared out of my head. For all I was worth, I could not take that first step.

My wife immediately called a Christian counseling group in town, and before long we were sitting in the reception room. I was back to my old tricks of looking for the nearest exit out of there should I start to panic. I was no longer in control. I had to wait for the receptionist to "turn green" and allow us to move.

We were ushered upstairs, and after only a few minutes with the counselor, the tears were pouring from my eyes. I was finally able to mourn for the passing of Jerry Falwell, and it was such a release. I was able go to work the next day and get back to a normal life. But it took the discharge of grief that was muzzled inside of me to allow me to get back to living.

As I said, over the years I had learned to allow emotions to be expressed. But those were your normal, everyday feelings that come along. My fear of average emotions had subsided.

When Jerry died, however, I think I wasn't ready for the magnitude of grief his death produced. I can see my subconscious kind of looking at that and saying, "Whoa, this is a little more than I'm prepared to handle. I wasn't banking on emotions of this scale."

My anxiety was caused by my subconscious not wanting to deal with the weight of grief that was holed up inside. So fear and anxiety tried to keep me in check so that it didn't have to deal with momentous emotions that were trying to surface.

During those few weeks after Jerry's death, each time I took that first step, I was telling my anxiety that I wasn't listening. I was moving on. And with each first step, I was also getting that much closer to experiencing the grief I was subconsciously trying to avoid. This was all happening in areas of my mind that were hidden to me. I wasn't aware of the battle at the time. It is only looking back that I can see how it all went down.

Finally, on the morning when I couldn't get out of bed, my fear was screaming at me. The grief was right there, ready to be released. My fear was shouting, yelling, commanding me to go no farther. It was not negotiating, it was dictating as best it could that I was to stay in bed and move no closer to my grief. My fear was not about to compromise on this.

Instead, I took another first step, this time not to fulfill my responsibilities, but to go get some help. And a few minutes with the Christian counselor allowed the grief to take its last step to expression.

It's like a volcano before it erupts. The pressure below the ground mounts, increasing little by little, the magma inching closer and closer to the surface. The rocks on top (my fear) try to maintain control over the escalating pressure. The magma (my emotions of grief) wants to be released. With each step I take, the magma of my grief moves closer to expression. The rocks of my fear increase its pressure to maintain control of the magma. Finally, when the magma (my grief) is at the point of breaking through, the rocks (fear) make one final plea for control. I take the first step out of that situation, essentially telling my fear to take a hike, and my volcano explodes releasing the pressure.

Such is the battle of someone who has grown up hating emotions, denying their existence, suppressing them into the depths of their being. It's not easy to reverse that kind of thinking, but it's as necessary as much as it's worth it.

In the aftermath of this crisis time, I began noticing something, especially in church. I'd be sitting in a church service during praise and worship and I'd see other Christians able to really let loose and just freely give themselves over to worshiping God. I didn't understand how they could do that. It seemed to me like they had no conscience. They had no shame. They were not the least bit held back by their status as sinners. They acted with no reservations and I wondered why I couldn't be like that. At times, I would stand there during praise and worship and be really, really angry because I wasn't able to worship God like others did.

It was a spiritual rehash of my teen years when I wondered why I couldn't ask a girl for a date, or go to a party, or engage in most social activities. I was frustrated in my past, and I was frustrated, developing an anger at this time as well.

I was jealous, even antagonistic toward those who were so flippant to think that they could be so transparent with God. How dare they be so arrogant? How outrageous they are to think that they have some special rapport with God. It seemed like they were not hindered in any way by their past. I was being hindered by something, but I wasn't sure what. I hated seeing other Christians able to be so free in their worship when I wasn't allowed that same freedom. I saw it as a sort of spiritual favoritism that some Christians were afforded this first class privilege while ones like me were stuck in the back of the plane. I felt slighted, trivialized, unimportant. It just seemed so unfair that I wasn't in the same league as those other Christians. I hated it, yet the more I saw, the more I knew that's what I wanted.

Learning how I felt about Jerry Falwell as a father figure to me after his death brought a realization that I did not have that same kind of perception of my Heavenly Father. To me, the Heavenly Father was aloof, detached, unaffected by my struggles. He was someone who had to be coaxed into action. He was wearied by my coming to Him with problems or situations that I faced. My paraphrase of Romans 8:32 went something like this:

"He who did not spare His own Son, but delivered Him up for us all, what else does He have to do? What else do you want from Him? What more does He need to do to make you happy?"

To me God blessed out of duty. He only gave because He said He would. He said that if I called on His name that He would save me, so He did. There was no passion, no desire, no love that motivated Him. He simply did what He said He would do because He said He would do it. It was a matter of benign commitment on His part, a dutiful execution of responsibilities He had promised to fulfill centuries before. I could envision Him in heaven answering prayers with a yawn saying, "Okay, I did say that I would do that, so here it is." Even the giving of Jesus on the cross was an act of duty, not desire.

In my mind, Jesus went to the cross simply because His Father asked Him to. There was no desire involved. There was no love involved. There was no emotion involved. Jesus died on the cross out of duty to His Father, because

His Father asked Him to. He was just being obedient.

I felt like I was just too much trouble for God. I wasn't worth the price that He paid on the cross. I felt like Jesus looked at me, then looked at what He suffered on the cross, and concluded that He overpaid for me.

I had no understanding of the true nature of my Heavenly Father. I had even less understanding of my position as His child and what benefits that entailed. I felt unworthy, unlovely, far too shameful to approach God in the way I saw other Christians approach Him. The nine year old boy who cringed at the thought of being loved was still alive. In essence, I couldn't let go of who I was before the cross was applied to my life. My past had a stranglehold on me and wasn't about to release its grip willingly. The idea of forgiveness was alien to my way of thinking. I just couldn't perceive that forgiveness was total, complete, freely given with no payment on my part. Those were foreign concepts to me.

What is the greatest distance known to man? Is the greatest distance the expanse of nothingness between planets, star systems, or galaxies? I contend that the greatest distance known to man is not in the vastness of space, it is the eighteen inches between the head and the heart. It's the route that truth must navigate if we are to experience God to the fullest. But it's a route filled with thieves that try to ambush any truth trying to make the journey, potholes ready to swallow up any truth bold enough to step out, twists and turns meant to steer truth in the wrong direction.

We can know things in our head, be absolutely convinced of the truths of the Bible intellectually, but to have those truths sink into the heart can be quite another matter. Knowing in the head is poles apart from understanding in the heart. I knew in my head that God was no respecter of persons, meaning that what was available for one was available for all. But inside that made no sense. I couldn't get past my guilt feelings. My self-assessment was shouting my unworthiness to me. How could I get past all of that?

How could I achieve the transformation from who I currently saw myself to be to who I was in reality in Christ. How could I attain the kind of freedom to worship that I observed in others?

I started by joining up with the recovery group in our church called "Freedom Ministry." I learned that people need to recover from a lot of things, not just drugs and alcohol. Painful pasts, divorce, and loss through death are just a few of the obstacles in our lives that require recovery. It was here where I discovered that my view of my heavenly Father was not at all representative of who the Father really was. He was not someone who forgave grudgingly. Instead, dispensing forgiveness to men was a priority for Him – dispensing forgiveness to ME was a priority for Him. He will never call back to memory things from our past that cause guilt feelings to return. He'll never make fun of us or ridicule us for the stupid things that we often do. He is kind, forgiving, gentle. All we have to do is read 1 Corinthians 13 and realize that the characteristics of love that we read about there are actually a description of God. So how was I to make the transition from who I thought God was to who God really was? It is through understanding who God is that we understand who we are.

I began by reading the gospels exclusively. For over a year that's the only part of the Bible I read. I ignored references to the Father as much as I could and focused my attention on who Jesus was. The word "father" didn't have the best connotations for me, so I took the advice of Jesus to Philip in John 14 when He said, "He who has seen me has seen the Father." I thought if I could get a good grasp on who Jesus was then I could transfer that understanding to the Father because Jesus and the heavenly Father have the same characteristics.

Do any of us really understand the Father completely? Are any of us totally free from misconceptions about the Father? I'd say we all can learn things about the Father that we don't know now. After all, this search for understanding is likely to be our main vocation in Heaven so we might as well get used to it now

CHAPTER 8

THE PRODIGAL'S FATHER

Your father is lounging in his recliner after a delightful dinner, catching up on the day's news. You're a little nervous as you secure your seat on the sofa. You have a question you want to ask him, but you're waiting for the right time. The nightly newscast is spewing out the worst the world had to offer that day and you decide that now is not that time. After a diet of violence, corruption, and politics, the news gives way to other, less irritating evening programming. Your nervousness grows because you sense that the time for your question is approaching. It isn't long before you decide that now is as good as it gets so you rise up, cross the room, give him a big hug, and pop the question.

"Dad, could I get my share of the inheritance now?"

After you help him back into his chair, he looks at you with a face that conveys the sense of someone who doesn't know what hit him. Now you wonder if you're going to get hit, only there will be no mystery about where it came from.

I can imagine a host of comebacks, all resulting in a simple two-letter word – no. How would your dad react to this question? Mine would lower his chin so he could look at me over top of his glasses. He would stare at me in disbelief for a few seconds and then raise his chin back up as he calmly uttered his two-letter answer. That would be the extent of our dialogue that evening.

Perhaps your dad would pick up the phone and set up an appointment with his estate lawyer to make a change in his will.

Maybe he would serenade you with a big belly laugh and thank you for bringing humor into the house that evening. Then as you leave the room, you anticipate the time in a day or two when he will speak to you again.

If my kids asked that question of me, I would pull out my wallet, hand them a twenty and tell them not to spend it all in one place.

How many fathers would seriously consider fulfilling such a request? What dad would give in and turn over his hard-earned money to the insolent little brat who couldn't wait for him to die? That dad would be crowned the king of milquetoast fathers.

Yet we read about just such a father in Luke chapter 15. The younger of his two sons came to him one day asking for his portion of the inheritance. How insulting! This son was apparently dissatisfied with the state of his family and his position in it. He wasn't happy where he was and obviously already had plans in place to leave and make his own way in the world. He was arrogantly disrespectful to his father in making his request.

This parable says a lot about the son, but it imparts to us much more about the father. As someone who had always had an inaccurate concept of my Heavenly Father, what I've learned here has helped me to understand my misconceptions and correct them.

It's obvious that the relationship between this younger son and the father was not a healthy one. There were problems that must have prompted the son to want to go where the grass is greener, to another country distancing himself from his home.

Did this father have the backbone of a jellyfish? He appears unable to refuse his youngest son's brazen demand. I can imagine that the son walked away from this encounter snickering at his father's inability to stand up to him. What a wimp, he must have thought. And yet was this father as weak as he appears to be on the surface? Let's look a little closer at this parable.

He must have amassed enough of a fortune to make it worth the son's efforts to ask for it. If this father's portfolio consisted of a few sheep, some crops, maybe a coin or two, and perhaps a small piece of land, what good would that be to this son who had grandiose plans to live it up in some far country. Such a small inheritance would have fallen well short of funding a journey like the one the son was contemplating.

This father was not at all poor. When the son came to the end of himself, he began reminiscing about his father's numerous servants, so he must have owned enough land or flocks to keep these servants busy. He had the money to feed all of his servants and treat them well enough for this son to yearn for the bread that they ate. The father's clothes closet was not barren because when the son came home he was adorned with the "best" robe and sandals. There was jewelry lying around the house because they put a ring on the son's finger upon his return. Livestock was not an issue since they killed the "fatted calf" for the joyous feast that marked the son's homecoming. When the elder son came in from the field and neared the house he heard music and dancing, so the father was able to hire musicians for the party, and the house was large enough to handle the crowd.

Since this father had the wherewithal to accumulate the wealth for all of these things, it seems fair to conclude that he was not as spineless as he appears. He obviously had some moxie in the way of business acuity. All this begs the question of why. Why did this father give his inheritance to his son who was intent on leaving? Was he just weak, or was there another motive behind his madness?

A sanctified reading between the lines might give us some clues.

This son obviously had no respect for his father. He wanted to get out. There must have been friction between the two because a son who is obedient and respectful doesn't just flip the cards one day and turn nasty. Offensive behavior was probably the norm for this younger of the brothers.

Did the father finally decide that he had had enough and gave his son what he requested just to get him out of the house? Was he so fed up with how his prodigal acted that he figured the share of the inheritance was a small price to pay for some peace? When the son left, did the father plop down on the hammock and inhale the newly found tranquility? Was the father glad that the rebellious son was gone? The father's actions when the son does finally return home indicates the opposite. On the return trip, as the son topped the final little hill before reaching the old homestead, the father saw him. Even though it was still some distance, the father knew immediately that it was his youngest son coming home. The simple fact that the father saw him a long way off implies that he was periodically scanning the horizon, longing for that first glimpse of a familiar figure walking toward him.

When the son did finally reappear on the horizon, he was probably walking slowly, shoulders hunched, head sagging, seriously withered from his bad experience. When the father spotted his wayward son, what did he do? We would all understand if he had planted himself on the front porch, awaited the son's final steps home, and demanded an explanation for his behavior. It would not be unreasonable for the father to question his son about why he was returning and what reason he had for asking to come back home. Certainly the father could reasonably take his son back in, but require him to meet some conditions in order to regain the trust he had squandered.

No one would question any of those scenarios had the father chosen to do so. But that's not what the father did at all. The instant he saw his son coming, he ran toward him with all that his aging body could give him. Some who study such things tell us that in order to run, the father had to hitch up his clothing to free up his legs. It was considered indignant for a grown man to behave in such a manner, but the father's love for his son superseded any shame others might impound to him.

I can imagine that when the time came for Jesus to be born, Jesus stood, hitched up His heavenly clothing and ran to the manger in the form of a baby so that thirty-three years later He could die our death.

When the father finally reached his son he hugged and kissed him with a kind of fervor reserved for those one loves. The father barely let his son speak. The prepared speech formulated in the pig sty of the foreign country fell on deaf ears, not because they were words that the father didn't want to hear, but because they were words he didn't need to hear. The son had probably rehearsed his lines a thousand times trying to develop just the right delivery so that his father would believe his sincerity. He never got to finish. The father was so happy to see him that words were unnecessary.

The son was restored to the position of sonship that he had the day he was born. All that had occurred between his birth and his return was forgotten like it never happened. The father reestablished the son's status in the family fully with no repercussions for the events that had transpired. The restoration was complete and unconditional. The son was back in the family with all the benefits of that relationship fully engaged.

Likewise, our Heavenly Father expects nothing from us when we turn to Him for salvation. There are no atoning actions needed or possible that would make us good enough for God to save us. A repentant heart is the only condition for salvation. As soon as we offer up to God such a heart, he runs to us as we appear on the horizon, puts His arms around us, accepts us altogether just as we are, and bestows upon us all the rights and privileges of sonship. The past is a non-factor, never to be visited again.

The relationship between the father and his youngest son was now the way it was meant to be. Is this what the father was seeking when he gave the son his share of the inheritance? If the relationship between the two had been healthy and satisfying, the son wouldn't have been so anxious to leave. Obviously, there was friction. The son must have developed, for whatever reason, a bitter or acidic attitude toward his father. He had become dissatisfied with the home life and wanted to get away as soon as possible.

What if the father had declined his son's request for the inheritance? Would anything have changed in the family? Would the son's unsavory attitude have continued, probably becoming worse over time? Would the discontent within the family have remained, perhaps poisoning the attitudes of the entire household?

Psalm 106:15 says, "{God} gave them their request, but sent leanness into their soul." The old saying says, be careful what you ask for. You might get it. Perhaps this parable teaches that sometimes God gives us what we want to bring us to the point of wanting what we need. This father of the prodigal knew that things weren't right and that something needed to happen to bring about correction. Giving his younger son what he wanted was the vehicle to bringing peace back into the family and his son back into the fold.

I remember when my son was eighteen years old. He was just a few months past his high school graduation and he was contemplating moving to Nashville, Tennessee with some of his friends. This was seven long hours of driving from our house in Virginia and my wife and I had the normal parental concerns about the idea. But we were supportive that if this is what he wanted to do, we would stand behind him all the way. In September of his high school graduation year, we loaded up and headed to Nashville.

This was one of the hardest things I have had to do. My imagination went into overdrive inflicting on my brain all kinds of awful scenarios of struggle my son would have to endure, and me not being there to help him. It wasn't like he was going off to college where there was at least some structure and support. He was going out on his own.

I wonder what this father was thinking as he watched his youngest son disappear over the horizon with his head held high, chest out, high-stepping along the dirt road, maybe whistling a little traveling tune. I imagine he couldn't take his eyes off the figure fading into the distance and prayed for his safe return. The sadness must have been intense.

What was our Heavenly Father thinking when he watched Adam and Eve walk away from the utopia called the Garden of Eden and toward a future of suffering and struggle?

Luke 15 is really a description of the father, not just the father of the story, but the Father of all fathers, the one who loves us with an everlasting love. When Adam and Eve left Eden, I think God the Father was thinking about a time far into the future when a cross would be the avenue for mankind to return. Just like the father of the prodigal looked for his son's return from the moment he left, the

Heavenly Father looked to the time when His Son would make it possible for all of us to be restored to a relationship with Him.

I've heard some commentators say that the reason God expelled Adam and Eve from the garden is so that they couldn't eat from the tree of life. Had they been able to eat from that tree, then they could have lived forever, but in a state of everlasting sin. God loved them, and us, too much to allow us to stay in our sin without the possibility of salvation.

This story of the prodigal is actually the third story in Luke 15, and the three are related. Each tells the tale of something that was lost and regained. They are all in response to a complaint made by the Pharisees that Jesus was showing kindness to sinners and sharing meals with them. Jesus proceeded to explain through these stories that these sinners were the reason He was there, that He had come to find what had been lost in the Garden of Eden.

The first two stories are similar in nature. In the first, Jesus asks rhetorically if there was a man there who, if he had lost one of his hundred sheep, wouldn't search exhaustively until he found it and brought it home. The obvious answer is that everyone there would do just that, track down the lost sheep and bring it back to safety.

The second story portrays a woman with ten coins. She misplaces one of the coins somewhere in the house. She lights a lamp and sweeps the dirt from every crack and corner of the house diligently, not quitting until she finds it.

The reaction of these two individuals is exactly the same. They call their friends and neighbors inviting them to celebrate the recovery of their lost item.

Then Jesus likens the joy of these people and their friends to the kind of joy that graces Heaven when just one sinner repents and turns his life over to God. What is the source of that joy? Based on the three stories in Luke 15 it would seem to come from the one who lost the object in the first place, the man and his sheep, the woman and her coin, and the father of the prodigal. In the case of the sinners that Jesus was communing with, that would be the Heavenly Father. Jesus is explaining to the Pharisees that He is spending time with these sinners because their recovery brings great joy to His Father in Heaven.

It is in this third parable of the chapter where we learn some details about this joy. What does the joy resulting from a repentant sinner look like? What attributes does it have? The story of the prodigal illustrates in more detail the kind of joy the Heavenly Father experiences when one of His love objects lost at the forbidden tree in the garden returns at the cross.

Anticipatory.
Both the man with the lost sheep and the woman who lost the coin were anticipating their success. There is no indication that either of them was going to give up until they found what they were looking for. From the moment of the loss, they expected their efforts to end up in victory. Likewise, the father of the prodigal began looking for his son's return immediately after releasing his gaze of the retreating figure over the horizon.

The Heavenly Father has been anticipating the homecoming of his love objects from the very beginning. While He was handing out the consequences of eating the forbidden fruit, He also announced the solution to the problem that had just been created. In Genesis 3:15 he prophesied to the serpent that there was coming a seed of the woman who would deal a death blow to his head.

After Adam and Eve blew it, God didn't return to the drawing board. He didn't hang His head and slink back to the throne room of Heaven to lick His wounds or mope over His misfortune. Instead He immediately published for the whole universe to hear that He was going to pave the way for His love objects to come back to Him. From that moment until now, God has been like the prodigal's father, watching the horizon, anticipating the return of any and all who would accept His provision of restoration.

Compassionate.

We can be judgmental at times when we see someone who is emerging from a difficult time in their lives, especially if it was partially due to their own actions. Maybe they hooked up with the wrong crowd, or strayed into habits that were harmful to them. It's easy to look down on someone who has wandered away and feel a little bit of spiritual snobbery that we stayed on the straight and narrow. There was no such reaction from the father of this story, nor is that the reception our Heavenly Father gives to His loved ones returning in repentance. Compassion is the only response our Heavenly Father bestows upon a repentant heart.

How many times do we read in the gospels where Jesus had compassion on a person or group? It didn't matter how exhausted He was from the obligations of the day. As soon as He saw someone in need, or a gathering of people desperate for a Shepherd, He responded with compassion. There was no hesitation or procrastination. Jesus didn't tell people that it was past His quitting time. He never advised anyone to take two spirit aspirins and come back in the morning. He took care of the need right then and there.

Immediate.

In this story, the father's compassion resulted in immediate action. This aging adult immediately ran to his son. There is no record of indecision or of second guessing himself. Surely, he could have waited at the gate of the homestead to greet his returning offspring. Instead the father rushed up the road to embrace his son and walk by his side for the last few yards of the journey home.

So it is when a sinner comes back to God. God does not call a meeting of the board of angels to discuss the situation. He has no "restoration committee" with a list of requirements that must be met before one of God's love objects can be accepted into the fold. There are no other pressing matters commanding His attention. God's repentance phone does not have a "hold" button. As soon as one of His love objects repents, God responds by running to the repentant sinner, putting His arms around him, and leading him home.

Unconditional.

Clearly, as the prodigal's father, he was entitled to an explanation as to why his son behaved the way he did. He was also completely within his rights to demand an accounting of what happened to all the money. No one would have faulted him if he had developed a list of conditions that the son would have to fulfill before being restored into the family. He did no such thing.

Neither does our Heavenly Father have a list of conditions that we need to fulfill in order to be accepted into His family. Indeed, we are summarily reminded many times, (Romans 3, Ephesians 2, to name just two) that there is nothing we can do to merit even a fraction of one percent of our salvation. We are justified by faith, not by works. Our greatest abilities account for nothing when it comes to salvation.

Complete.

The father of the prodigal restored to his son all the rights and privileges a son should have. He held nothing back. Restoration was without reservation. All relationships were fully repaired. The son had the same position within the family that he had the day he was born.

God's salvation goes all the way. It covers everything. Nothing slips through the cracks. There is no backburner item to be dealt with later. All of our sin is gone, every last morsel of iniquity in our lives is eradicated. The righteousness of Christ permeates our being, envelops our souls. God sees nothing but good as far as our relationship with Him is concerned. All is as it was meant to be.

It amazes me that all of these characteristics were exhibited when I became a Christian. I was a nonentity. I was a zero in relationships, abilities, and potential. I was traveling down the road of worthlessness, destined for nothingness. All the things that described me in the previous chapters were all there was for God to see. I had nothing to offer in exchange for a home in Heaven.

Yet when I turned by heart toward God, my Heavenly Father felt all the characteristics of the joy detailed for us in Luke 15. That is astounding! It just overwhelms me! It's hard to find the words to adequately explain how much God wanted me when I was nothing.

It is this understanding of how God responded to me so incredibly when I became a Christian that has been instrumental in turning my faulty view of who He is around. It's a work in progress, but it is happening.

CHAPTER 9

BELIEFS

September 11, 2001. Just another normal work day for millions of Americans, scurrying about offices, tending to customers' needs, transporting goods across the country, that is until around ten o'clock that morning.

I had just gotten back into my car after delivering a tape to one of our producers at his house. As soon as I started the car, the announcer on the Christian radio station came on in a very somber voice, asking everyone to pray for what was happening in New York. He didn't say what had happened, and I conjectured about it being a mass transit accident or some sort of shooting. When I got back to the studio and saw the smoke coming out of the twin towers, I joined the rest of America in trying to make sense of what I was seeing. Needless to say, my desire for work dissipated, and I was magnetized to the news reports for the rest of the day.

This event changed me, as it did most Americans. Consider all those people who actually lost someone in the attack. The murder of loved ones and friends disrupted families forever. We all asked, why did this happen?

The answer, because of a belief system. A few Middle Eastern men believed something about their god and how they could please him. They believed that their god was the one and only. They believed that anyone who didn't worship the same god as they did were infidels and therefore deserving to die. They believed they were doing their god's work by killing these infidels. They also believed that there would be a great reward in heaven if they were to die as martyrs.

Not only did they believe these things, they believed them strongly. These weren't just off the cuff discussions as they sipped lattes at the corner coffee shop. It wasn't a small diversion while they watched a soccer match on television. It consumed them. They were serious. They were committed. They were passionate, and that passion translated into actions.

I can imagine that their last moments before the planes hit the twin towers were marked by a high anticipation of eternal reward. They were convinced that they were doing the right thing. Their belief system allowed them, even instructed them to kill in the name of their god, and be excited about it. Their belief was more important than life itself.

Such misguided conviction is repugnant to me, but it illustrates how important our beliefs are, to the extent of determining who we are as persons.

My grandparents believed in freedom. They lived in the Ukraine region of Russia in the early part of the twentieth century and experienced the Communist takeover. Individual rights were erased. My grandfather was a successful businessman, but suddenly everything became the property of the state. One day he was supporting his family, the next, he was supporting the Communists.

My grandparents had a belief system of their own. They believed that if they could make it to the United States, they would have the opportunity to live their lives the way they wanted. They believed that their children would have greater opportunity in America than they would have under the Communists. They believed in the ideals of freedom that America espoused, and their belief was so strong that they risked everything to get to that freedom.

This was no small undertaking because it wasn't just my

grandfather and grandmother. They had three children at the time. They carefully planned their escape. My grandmother sewed money into the lining of her dress to be used to bribe the guards at the border. The risk was tremendous. What if someone along the journey turned them in to the authorities? What if the border guards couldn't be bribed? What if they came across loyal Communist soldiers who discovered what they were doing? If at any time during their smuggling operation they were exposed, they would have been separated from their children, possibly never to see them again, an agonizing prospect in and of itself. They would probably have spent significant time in prison. It was a tremendous sacrifice they made so that they, their children, and my cousins and I, could live in a free country.

They lived in Ankara, Turkey for six months until they could get sponsorship to the U.S. They then boarded a boat, crossed the Atlantic, and sailed into New York harbor. I can't imagine what it was like to get that first glimpse of Lady Liberty waving her welcome. What feelings of anticipation filled them at that moment? It must have been like waking up from a nightmare to a new and exciting reality.

Two groups of people. Two sets of beliefs. Two avenues of actions based on those beliefs. Two very different results.

Beliefs are a strong motivation to actions.

What is it that causes belief to result in action? Why do two people who believe the same thing have different levels of response to their belief? Why did my grandparents have the fortitude to navigate from Russia to the United States while others in the same situation, who may have been just as disgusted with the new government, resigned themselves to life under Communism?

The answer lies in that longest voyage in the universe – the eighteen inches from the head to the heart. The heart is commonly referred to as the seat of the emotions. It is where our feelings originate. It is where our motivation to action comes from. If we don't feel it, we are likely not to do it. We talk about being stirred into action. We can believe that it's the right thing to donate time to a charity, but if we don't feel the urge, we are less inclined to actually put feet to our belief.

For the most part as human beings, what we feel is what we do. Certainly there are those times when we might feel like applying the right fist of understanding to the jaw of someone in need of learning, but we don't because we can foresee spending some quality time with a judge. The threat of consequences will sometimes prevent us from doing what we feel like doing. But in the normal course of life we tend to do things only to the extent that we feel like doing things. The stronger we feel something, the more likely we will be stirred into action.

What we're talking about here is the difference between knowledge and understanding. Knowing something is not the same as understanding something.

I have never had a desire to learn about cars and what makes them run. All I know about a car engine is that when I put my key in the ignition and turn it, the engine starts. I know nothing about why it happens, just that it does. When I open the hood with a wrench in my hand, I hear the engine crying out to its mama for protection. It would be a tragedy for me to attempt to fix a problem. The result would end up as the central exhibit in the "Mechanics Museum of What Not To Do To An Engine."

The mechanic who works on my car is in a much different position. He can explain exactly what transpires when the ignition is turned. He can tell you why the engine starts, not just that it does. When he opens the hood with a wrench in his hand, the engine starts purring because it knows that it's going to feel better real soon.

The difference between the two of us is that my mechanic understands the engine. I simply know that it exists. My mechanic can perform all kinds of surgeries on an engine. I can't give it an aspirin. My mechanic can take an engine apart and put it back together with everything in its right place. If I tried to reassemble an engine, I could probably make some money selling it as a modern art sculpture.

I know, but my mechanic understands. That understanding allows him to do things I would never dream of trying. He can act on his understanding. My simple knowledge is not nearly enough for me to be of any use in fixing an engine.

In the spiritual world of Christianity, understanding results in action. Simple knowledge often does not.

The prom is just weeks away. Two guys are anticipating the event. One surveys the female landscape during school to determine which lucky lady will be privileged to spend the evening with him. The other dreads it. He hates the pressure it brings. Every overheard conversation about the prom reminds him that he's too scared to ask a girl to go with him. And God forbid that for some unexplainable reason a girl would ask him to the prom.

As the day of the event approaches, the first guy's excitement builds. The second guy just plugs along unable to join in. He can't wait until the prom is over so he won't feel so inferior to his classmates.

The second guy in the above example, of course, is me. I absolutely hated special social events in high school. They only reinforced the inferiority I always felt when I compared myself to my classmates. I could never get involved, no matter how much I really wished I could be like everyone else.

Why? What was the difference between the guy who got a date for the prom and me, the one whose feet were as cold as absolute zero?

The difference is what each of us believed about ourselves. The first guy believed that he was worthy of a girl's attention. I didn't. The first guy believed a girl would find a date with him to be fun. I believed any girl would rather stay home than go to the prom with me.

Those beliefs turned into feelings. My beliefs dictated my feelings of inferiority which resulted in my lack of action. The other guy felt confidence and positive anticipation of a fine evening with a member of the opposite sex.

Being the social misfit that I was as a teenager, I believed that no girl in their right mind would go with me to the prom. The feeding of the five thousand was a dinner for two compared to the miracle that would have been required for me to have a date for the prom. Because of my belief, I felt inferior to other guys who were asking girls for dates all around me. Those feelings of inferiority influenced my resulting action of not asking for a date.

It was kind of a vicious cycle. Belief, followed by feeling, followed by action – or inaction – resulting in a reinforcement of my beliefs. My belief resulted in my feelings, which influenced my actions, or lack thereof, which only served to confirm that my assessment of myself was correct – I was not worthy a girl's attention.

How frustrating it is to know what you should be able to do, and not be able to do it. It eats at you until you just quit trying. But what to do about it

CHAPTER 10

THE PAST

It was the middle of a summer night in our old farmhouse that had no air conditioning. I was asleep in my upstairs bedroom with the windows open hoping there would be a nighttime breeze flowing. The head of my bed was nestled against one of the windows, through which I could access the roof over our front porch if I wished. I placed my pillows on the actual window sill to get as close to the cool night air as possible. A window screen separated me from the myriad of bugs that populated the farm.

It was during one of these nights, about two or three in the morning, when a thunderstorm rolled over the farm. The cool rain was a welcome relief, especially when the splashes from the drops hitting the porch roof filtered through the screen onto my face. I usually didn't wake up very often during these storms, but this one was different. I was jolted to consciousness by one particular bolt of lightning, and the resultant thunder clap that seemed to originate right there in my room. It was really loud! I couldn't see the barn from the window, but what I did see was something I had never seen before and probably will never see again.

I immediately opened my eyes and witnessed a massive shower of sparks hurtling at least two hundred feet away from the barn. They weren't small and there weren't just a few. The waterfall of orange colored sparks lit up the entire area, and then they were gone. The fiery outburst lasted less than five seconds, but it got my attention - at least for a moment.

THE ISOLATION ROOM

I bolted up immediately and woke my dad to tell him what I saw, right? Not exactly. I went right back to sleep and told him what I had seen at the breakfast table the next morning. He was always a very sound sleeper and hardly anything ever woke him up, even thunder from a hundred feet away. He adamantly expressed his desire that I should have awakened him as soon as it happened.

After breakfast we went outside to a barn that was still standing. A thorough inspection revealed that the lightning bolt had entered at the peak of the roof, seared its way down one of the wooden support beams, and exited at the bottom of the roof, all of which was on the second floor of the barn. A brown stripe running the length of the beam was the telltale sign.

Being summertime, we had recently harvested some hay and it was piled high within twenty feet of the lightning's path. Little did I realize when I woke up to see those sparks that we could have been seconds away from having the bonfire of the century. Why the barn or its contents never caught fire is still a mystery.

But that's not the end of the story. One poor soul was unfortunate enough to be in the wrong place at the wrong time, and that was our dog. There was a forebay, essentially a concrete porch running the entire length of the barn. We attached a chain at each end of the forebay so our dog could run back and forth all day if he wanted. Several doors from the forebay opened into various areas of the barn's first floor, one opening to the location of our doghouse where our dog spent his nights. The place where the lightning exited was just above his bedroom. Can you imagine the fright that he felt when lightning struck just ten feet above him?

Our dog's actions after that harrowing experience gives an insight into one of the factors influencing our beliefs, namely our past. After that night, if our dog heard thunder, no matter how distant it was, he'd come out onto the forebay and look toward the house with imploring eyes, begging for us to come get him and take him into the house until the storm passed. He wanted no part of another lightning strike. We may not have heard any thunder ourselves, but if we saw our dog pleading for deliverance, we knew there was a storm somewhere in the distance.

In this respect, we have something in common with animals. Past experiences can affect present behavior. On the negative side, perhaps we have a fear of heights because we once fell out of a tree. I got knocked down by a German Shepherd after school one day and had a fear of big dogs after that. On the positive side, as children we enjoy all the activities of the Christmas season, so as parents we do things that will give our children the same delights that we experienced. A camping trip either endears us to the outdoors or makes us vow to never spend another night in a tent as long as we live, depending on how many times mosquitos feasted on us. Events of our past do affect how we think and act in the present.

No one ever faulted our dog for his fearful behavior pattern. It was completely understandable that he would panic any time he heard distant thunder. He believed that danger was imminent and therefore sought for shelter inside the house. Our dog experienced trauma caused by the intense thunder, so from that point forward, whenever he heard even distant thunder, it brought back the terror of that night and he sought refuge.

This is how all animals are. They do what they do because they are what they are. When a shark senses blood in the water, he motors straight to it because that's his nature. When a spider catches a fly in its web, he rushes to encase it for later use as a meal. He doesn't ask whether the fly might have a wife and kids at home. There is no place for sentimentality. The spider does what he does because that's what spiders do. That's just the way it is in nature.

An animal can be justly excused from crude behavior because that's just the way he is. But we are not animals. We are human beings created by God with minds that can reason.

Our dog couldn't intelligently explain to himself that the lightning strike of that summer night was likely a once in a lifetime event. He couldn't logically sort through the long odds of a similar event happening again. He never heard the saying that lightning never strikes twice in the same place. All he knew was that he had experienced trauma which caused him to believe that he was in danger, and he wanted to escape from having that experience again. An experience in the past affected his behavior for the rest of his life. He never got over it.

As humans, a lot of what we do and who we are is erected on our past, and that is not necessarily bad. We base our vocation on our abilities and interests. Musical parents tend to instill their love for music in their children, who may become worship leaders or symphonic musicians. Athletes often come from parents who follow sports. A child who finds out early that he can hit a few baskets develops a love for basketball. What we find success in early often influences our vocations as adults. If we are good in math, we might become an engineer, programmer, or certified public accountant. If we have a creative imagination, we might get into the film or theater industry as directors or actors.

We all have certain tendencies in our personalities. A tender heart toward suffering might induce a career in counseling or humanitarian missions. An analytical nature lends itself to science or computer technology. Strong leadership qualities can lead to CEO's. A high tolerance for risk brings out entrepreneurs who start their own businesses. Some of these personality traits are inborn in us. Others are developed from influences during our formative years. These are not issues that require a lot of attention. They are just normal factors in our lives that help determine the course we take. It's all good.

But what about someone like me? I had developed a severe case of the "fears" as I was growing up which resulted in a full retreat from life. I spent eighteen months in self-imposed isolation honestly believing that if I were to be invisible to the human race, then everyone would be better off. I believed I was not worth the attention anyone might give to me. I believed that I was not worth getting to know as a person. I believed that I wasn't capable of worthwhile human interaction that included any discussion deeper than the weather. I believed that I was devoid of human emotions, so when conversations turned in those directions, I had nothing to offer.

Is all of that "just the way I was" and therefore set in stone? Was I the ultimate human dud because that's how God made me? Was I the person I was because that's just the way I was, and therefore I just needed to learn to live with it?

I became a Christian at the age of twenty. At that time I was blessed with a great future that includes a home in Heaven and the opportunity to see God in all His glory. I was guaranteed a future free from suffering, pain, or physical limitations. I was endowed with a future of joy, happiness, and peace. My future is awesome, and so is yours if you have placed your faith in Jesus Christ as your Savior.

All of that is great for the future, but do we have to

wait until they close the lid on our casket before we can experience any of that? Are all of those great things just in the future, or can we grab a taste of some of it while still here on earth? Was I relegated to a life of timidity and retreat, only to be released upon the day of my death? Was there no hope for change for someone like me?

If we are constrained by the kind of people we are to be that way for life, then what is the renewing of the mind of Romans 12 all about? Why does God say that we are new creatures in 2 Corinthians 5:17 if nothing new is possible? Does God save us and then just leave us to wallow in our humanness until the time that He takes us home? Why are we instructed to grow in Christ if no growth is possible?

Growth is an essential ingredient for a healthy Christian life. For people like me, growth is a matter of survival. I couldn't function normally in society the way I was. I had to change or I would have never been able to go to college, get married, have a family, hold down a job, or do anything that makes life worth living.

My retreat from society was the result of my belief that I was worth nothing as a human being. In order to break out of that mental prison, I had to change what I thought about myself. I had to revamp my image of myself so that I could reengage with people.

How did I do that? It started with an understanding of truth

CHAPTER 11

THE IMPORTANCE OF TRUTH

We've all seen the video. A house ringed by bushes and trees, clothed in beige siding with dark brown trim, a two-seater swing suspended from a wrap-around porch, the perfect place to experience those spring thunderstorms. Little gnome figurines encompassed by flowers of all colors separate the porch from the lush, green lawn which is dotted with brightly colored toddler toys left out in the rain. A hammock stretched between two small trees tempts all who pass by to take a nap. Even little Fido is pampered with a beige and brown doghouse. The scene is the poster child for peace and tranquility.

Then the camera zooms out and the perception of serenity is crushed. The video reveals a raging torrent of water that has carved a gully menacingly close to the edge of the house. Perhaps these are flood waters from a dam break, or an unusually wicked winter being released from its icy, mountaintop prison.

The videographer locks his lens on the volatile scene as he awaits the inevitable. Every minute, the distance between the house and the gully diminishes as masses of dirt are ousted from their abode after centuries of faithful service to the earth.

Before long, a small portion of the underside of the house is laid bare by the burglary of the ground underneath. The structure remains intact – for now, but the videographer won't have to wait much longer.

Then it happens. The decisive piece of terra firma is

ripped away and the house collapses into the torrent to be reunited at the bottom of the valley with the dirt it once rested upon.

It doesn't matter that the house was constructed with the best materials by the most qualified workmen and from a flawless design. Brick, stone, wood, whatever made up the structure was unable to survive when the base upon which it relied upon was no longer there.

Let's back up a few years. Imagine that you're strolling along the banks of the Sea of Galilee in northern Israel on a spring day admiring the great number of boats lightly skimming the smooth surface of this hallowed lake. Your thoughts are interrupted by a faint voice echoing at you from above. As you shade your eyes against the Middle Eastern sun you look up and see a throng of people adorning a hillside, each person focused on a man who is standing in their midst. Intrigued, you climb the hill to get close enough to hear what he is saying. He creates the impression of being some sort of teacher, commanding everyone's undistracted attention.

He speaks with authority as he talks about the qualities a person needs to be happy. He lectures on the kind of righteousness required to be counted worthy to enter Heaven. He instructs the people about how to treat their enemies, warns them not to be hypocrites, and follows with a discourse on how much God cares for them and wants to meet their needs. His audience remains attentive.

He continues by promoting a principle of treating others in the same way they themselves want to be treated, and then admonishes the gathering about the importance of being inwardly sincere, that outward righteousness is not enough. Just doing the right things is insufficient to warrant a place in Heaven. Righteousness must be internal.

He finishes his discourse by relating a scene similar to

the one documented by the videographer above. He compares two houses, one built on rock, the other on sand, both assailed by fierce storms. The one resting on rock withstood the best the tempest had to offer. It remained stable, secure, unmoved by the mightiest attacks thrown at it. The second house's fate was far different. As the wind and rain shifted the sand on which it rested, the house trembled at the fury. Eventually, because the foundation of sand beneath it became unstable, the house collapsed, and its demise was a terrible sight to see.

The person doing the teaching here, of course, was Jesus Christ, and today we call his words the Sermon on the Mount. What was Jesus teaching from this final illustration of the two houses? What was He conveying when he contrasted the foundations upon which the houses were resting? What do the rock and the sand represent?

We all know that sand is a rather easily disturbed commodity, to say the least. Sand pellets bombard our face as we walk the beach on a windy day. Enough wind and storm surge, and entire sand dunes are eradicated and must be rebuilt. The smallest child taking a walk on the beach can, with each footstep, leave behind a testimony of the stroll. The currents from the ocean waves constantly alter the topography of the sands beneath the surface. Any number of forces imposing their will on the sand is met with minor resistance.

Now, apply these same forces to a rock big enough to anchor a house. The rock yawns at a stiff breeze or strong wind. A hurricane or tornado induces not even the slightest reaction. Countless thousands of boots, shoes, and sandals may have traipsed over the surface leaving no trace. Water is helpless to inflict its will on this foundation on steroids.

Try burying yourself in a rock like you would the sand

on a beach. Even children with their toy shovels and pails erect sand castles that are overthrown by the next high tide.

What was Jesus referring to when he contrasted the rock and sand at the end of his sermon? What could these two substances with dissimilar characteristics have in common? Both were charged with the same responsibility, to be the foundation of a house. Both were bombarded by wind, rain, and flood. One excelled in its obligations, the other was a colossal failure. But they were both contracted for the same purpose, to support the houses erected on them.

What about the houses themselves? What do they symbolize? What kind of structures are they? Should we view them as literal, physical buildings, or are they something else?

Jesus had just completed the most famous sermon of His ministry on that hillside above the Sea of Galilee. He spent 102 verses teaching principles of spiritual living, how we should handle various situations that come our way in everyday life. He taught spiritual truth, spiritual values, and spiritual ideals to guide us on our journey through life. Then He talked about these houses suggesting that the two men who erected them were constructing their spiritual lives, and where they chose to build revealed how much importance they placed on the principles of the previous 102 verses. The man who built on the rock took those teachings seriously, recognizing that what Jesus taught formed a solid foundation. The man who built on the sand may have viewed the teachings of Jesus as nice suggestions, but also may have thought there were other belief systems just as valid.

In relating this little story about the houses, Jesus was raising an issue that has flustered many people throughout history. What do we do with the principles taught by God?

Are they suggestions or are they commands? Are they open to personal interpretation or are they to be followed no matter the situation? Are they sand or are they rock? Or, to use today's terminology, are they relative, meaning subject to change, or are they absolute, no changing possible?

The absoluteness of truth has been questioned from the very beginning. In the Garden of Eden the serpent raised doubts in the minds of Adam and Eve about the truth God had given them. "Did God really say…?" We all know how that turned out.

Numerous times throughout the Old Testament the phrase is written, "Every man did that which is right in his own eyes." The truth of God was neglected in favor of each person doing what they thought was right, not using the guidelines God had given them. In each case the results were less than favorable.

When Jesus was on trial before Pilate in John 18:37-38, Jesus stated that every person who is of the truth hears His voice. Pilate responded with the question whose answer has eluded mankind from the very beginning. Pilate asked, "What is truth?" I can't help but wonder if at that moment Pilate realized that he was staring truth in the face.

Truth has taken a real hit in today's world. It is mishandled, misunderstood, maligned, and misrepresented. It is ignored and ridiculed. It is twisted and spun. It is taken out of context to make it appear to support a certain opinion. It is accepted selectively, embracing that which is liked and discarding the rest. It is lamented as unable to be found, yet it may be the most sought after entity we know.

It is often quite aggravating to listen, especially in the news media, as people on various sides of an issue state their arguments. We have entered a time when we really don't know who we can trust. Are they giving us a true and complete picture of a particular topic, or just the parts they want us to hear? We have to be polished in the art of discernment to sift through the bombardments coming at us from all directions.

The old saying that beauty is in the eye of the beholder has been updated. Today, truth is in the eye of the beholder. We pick and choose what we want to believe, and essentially, it is those things that most closely fit in with our worldview. Any more, truth does not have an effect on our worldview, our worldview determines what truth we choose to believe. If something doesn't fit with our belief system, we ignore it, not caring if it is the truth or not.

We all have worldviews that determine what we believe. The question is this. Is our worldview our master or our servant? Do we give ourselves permission to alter our worldview when we are confronted with a nugget of truth that counters what we believe? In other words, when we come across a truth that conflicts with what we believe, do we treat that truth as a rock, or as silly putty? It depends on whether our worldview is our master or our servant.

If we are the master of our worldview, then we treat truth as a rock. When we take that truth and apply it to our worldview, our worldview will have to change its shape in some way to accommodate for the shape of the rock. It's like placing a stone in an area of mud. As we press the stone into the mud, the mud will give way, allowing the stone to embed itself. The mud makes room for its new resident. In this case, the worldview is malleable, and the truth is solid.

If, on the other hand, our worldview is our master, then we treat the truth as silly putty. We take the truth, mold it, reshape it, customize it, trying to make it fit into the form of what we believe. If it turns out that no amount of manipulation can make it conform to our worldview, then we toss it aside and ignore it. In this case, the truth is malleable and our worldview is solid and unmoving. In essence, our worldview is our master and we are its slave.

Nothing illustrates this more than the intellectual battle between evolution and creation. An abundance of truth is available for our consumption in the world today. Molecular structure, fossil records, the separation of species, these and a myriad of other things are scientifically unquestioned. They are the truths of how our world operates.

The question is this. Given the two theories of how our universe started, the two worldviews of Creation and evolution, which one does the scientific truths documented about our world fit in with better?

An honest assessment must conclude that the truths that have been verified scientifically fit in much better with Creation than evolution.

God created every creature "after its kind". Today, crossbreeding takes place within a species, such as a tiger and a lion, or a polar bear and a grizzly bear. But you can't crossbreed a cat with a dog, a cow with a monkey, etc. Species can only breed "after their kind".

The absoluteness of molecular structure cries out for a Creator. How can we be sure that the floor we are standing on won't gradually give way sending us into whatever is beneath? It's because the molecular structure of the wood or material under our feet is unchanging. We feel secure because we don't expect it to change.

We create medicines based on how chemicals interact with each other, and how those chemicals will affect things that are in our bodies. If evolution was in effect, how do we know that the medicine we take today will not be poison tomorrow? It's because chemical interaction is trustworthy. How chemicals react with each other will not change over time. We know and have proven that what we discover today will still be true tomorrow.

Just the absoluteness of our universe screams out against evolution. The precision of planetary orbits is amazing. The magnificence of how life cycles work is incredible. The marvelous way all of our bodily functions interact with each other is fascinating. My daughters both took Exercise Science in college. As I quizzed them for tests on the human anatomy, I was repeatedly amazed at the complexity and compatibility of the various systems of our bodies. Just the organization of how everything works together in our world hollers its support for Creation.

The odds of that organization in our world happening by evolutionary chance is so astronomical that to even consider such a thing to be true is ludicrous. But that's exactly what evolutionary scientists do. They start with the belief that evolution is fact. There is no questioning, no discussion. They scoff at the notion that Creation is even a possibility, and belittle those who believe Creation to be true.

So, every truth they discover must be integrated into their evolutionary belief system. No matter how hard it may be, they simply will not allow something they learn to alter their worldview. They will struggle, manipulate, reshape until they can somehow justify that the truth actually reinforces their view of evolution. For them, evolution is their unquestioned master and no amount of evidence, however compelling it might be, will supplant evolution from their belief system. If they simply cannot come up with an explanation, then they say, "we just don't understand it all yet", instead of acknowledging the possibility that they may be wrong.

What we've done today is to call things that support our position "the truth" while we call things that contradict our position "lies". We don't want to change how we think.

We don't want to be told that we are wrong. We can't stand the thought of altering our belief system to conform to truth. We instead shy away from, even run from, anything that might challenge our way of thinking.

I often wonder if this castration of truth isn't what Jesus was envisioning when He said in Luke 18:8, "When the Son of Man comes, will He really find faith on the earth?" People have faith in a lot of things these days, but Jesus is referring to His definition of faith, which is a faith in the truth of God.

The problem we all need to face is that there is such a thing as truth, and there are such things as lies. Truth is critical to the renewing of the mind. I spent my entire life believing lies about myself and about God. What if I tried to overcome a lie in my life, like my faulty view of God's character? Suppose I succeeded at one point of replacing that lie with the truth of who God is. What if, then, at some future time, that truth changed because the character of God changed, or God changed His mind about us? A truth that changes is a terrible thing to rely on. An unchangeable God is essential to overcoming the lies in our lives.

So what is truth? Some say that truth changes with the ages. What was truth for one generation is no longer valid for the next but must be adapted to reflect changes in society. It must be adjusted to adequately address new ideas, new concepts, or new discoveries in science and technology. Truth that worked decades and centuries ago must undergo reevaluation to keep up with the times.

Granted, scientific discoveries sometimes require us to alter our thinking about our world. We once thought the world was flat until science revealed that to be false. The truth didn't change, just our understanding of it. We once thought the sun revolved around the earth and that the earth was the center of the universe. Now we know that

THE ISOLATION ROOM

the earth is just one planet orbiting the sun, just a very small speck of real estate in the vastness of space.

What about truth? Does it exist? Is it important? Should we pay attention to it? Does it have any meaning for our lives?

Is there such a thing as absolute truth? Are there truths that are never-changing? Are there universal truths that apply to every person equally with no exceptions? Does absolute truth exist?

Ask the NASA engineer who has to make all the calculations for an upcoming launch. He ascertains the weight of the payload and rocket assembly, the thrust of the engine, the height of the orbit, and countless other factors. He must figure out how much fuel will be needed to reach orbit. There are many variables to consider in order to propel a satellite into orbit. But there is one factor that he can trust and that is gravity. It is a constant in the equation. Pity the poor guy if he had to guess at how much force the earth's gravitational field would exert on the day of the launch. What if the gravitational force today differed from two months from now when the launch is scheduled? What if his calculations from today were unreliable when it came time for liftoff? Every launch would be a crap shoot.

But gravity is constant. Gravity is reliable. Gravitational pull does not change from day to day. It is absolute. It will not change and its effect on each person is the same. We all have the same gravitational factors to contend with as we move on the earth, no exceptions.

Physical laws are unchanging. Energy equals mass times the speed of light squared, the speed of light being an absolute mathematical constant.

It's been a long time since I took Chemistry in high school, but I remember doing experiments. The teacher would tell us to mix chemical A with chemical B and we were to report on what happened. We worked in groups and each group performed the same operation. Isn't it amazing that no matter how many times the experiments were done, and how many different people or groups did them, the results were always the same. The morning class results were the same as the afternoon class results. The results on Tuesday were the same as the results on Wednesday. The results one year were the same as the results the previous year. That's because the chemicals had certain properties that never changed, and the teacher knew when he constructed the experiment what the results would be. There was never any variation.

All throughout the physical universe there are absolutes that we can trust. There are absolutes all around us that will never change. God can vary physical laws to suit His purposes, but we can do nothing to change them ourselves.

That is true of the physical universe we call our home, but what about the "moral" universe. What about those principles that guide our conduct? Are there absolute moral laws that will not, indeed cannot change?

If all we do is look at the mess our world is in, the answer would seem to be in the negative. Wars, crime, cruel dictatorships, ethnic cleansing, and a myriad of other maltreatments of the human race would seem to indicate that such absolute moral edicts do not exist. Gravity is not given a choice whether to be active on any given day. It cannot choose to renege on its responsibility to keep us humans attached to the ground. Its pull is always there and nothing we do can change it. But it seems like we humans can make all kinds of choices about how to conduct our lives. Just observing human behavior gives one the impression that our choices of moral conduct are innumerable, if not infinite.

But does that mean that there are no absolutes when it

comes to our moral universe? Is there no code of conduct that teaches us to act in a certain way each time we encounter a question of morality? Can we say with certainty that moral absolutes do not exist?

If we look at this question logically, not only can we conclude that moral absolutes probably do exist, we can prove that at least one moral absolute HAS to exist. It is impossible to say with honesty that there are no moral absolutes. To reject the existence of absolute moral truth is a denial of logic.

What is absolute truth? If we want to prove something, we probably should know what it is. Let's get very finite in our definition. There are two aspects to an absolute truth.

First, no influence, internal or external, has the power to alter it. An absolute truth is a truth that remains constant, unchanging, all-encompassing no matter what influences may assault it from within or without. Nothing can change it and it cannot change itself. An absolute truth has always, and will always exist in its current form.

Second, an absolute truth applies to every person in the world. Given a moral question, each one who encounters this question must be guided by this truth in making his or her determination on how to answer. An absolute truth bears weight on every person who would be confronted with this moral question.

In short, an absolute truth has never, and can never change, and applies equally to everyone who has to answer a given moral question.

An absolute truth is one that will never require an alteration in either action or conclusion. An absolute truth will be constant, consistent, unalterable. When an action and conclusion is determined once, then that action and conclusion will never have to change because the truth guiding them will never change.

Let's apply this to the moral universe. How does absolute truth work in the area of morality?

There's a mathematical and philosophical method of argumentation called "reductio ad absurdum." The "Internet Encyclopedia of Philosophy" gives the definition as follows:

"Reductio ad absurdum is a mode of argumentation that seeks to establish a contention by deriving an absurdity from its denial, thus arguing that a thesis must be accepted because its rejection would be untenable."
(https://www.iep.utm.edu/reductio/#H3

Putting it in layman's terms, you take a statement that you want to prove. You turn the statement around to its exact opposite and follow reasoning to prove the opposite's truth instead. If, when you reach your final conclusion you end up with a contradiction that simply cannot be dismissed, meaning that the "opposite" of the statement you are trying to prove simply cannot be correct, then you have proven that the original statement has to be true. That may be hard to follow right off, so let's take "reductio ad absurdum" and apply it to the issue of absolute truth.

The statement we want to prove is this; "There is absolute moral truth." We want to show that absolute moral truth must exist in our "moral universe." Using "reductio ad absurdum" we take the exact opposite of that statement and say the following; "There is NO absolute moral truth." Let's see where that leads us.

Let's suppose that there is a moral situation that we will label "Moral Situation A" (we'll use the acronym MSA). This could be a question of honesty, whether to lie about someone or not. It could be a dilemma involving how to react to someone who lies about us. Maybe it's even more serious such as a decision to become entangled in criminal activity. It could be any of a million moral circumstances that face the human race. Let's just take one of those moral questions and assume that there is no absolute truth, no constant guideline to help us in making our determination about what to do.

Here comes our first human to encounter this MSA, we'll call him "Person 1." This person is faced with some decisions. What should he do in response to MSA?

First, let's apply the "opposite" statement that we are trying to prove which is "There is no absolute moral truth." When formulating his opinions about this challenge of morality he finds that there is nothing concrete to guide him. There is no principle of thought of an absolute nature upon which to rely to make his decision. So, he uses what he has available which are his intellect, his environment, his life experiences, his opinions, anything that he can draw upon to determine his response to MSA. He can take all this input and accept what he wants and reject what he doesn't want. After careful thought he settles on a plan of action and goes along his merry way.

Not long after "Person 2" stumbles on the same MSA. Again we employ our "opposite" statement that there is no absolute moral truth available for guidance, so Person 2 utilizes his experiences, intellect, environment, and opinions which are undoubtedly differ somewhat from those of Person 1. He therefore formulates his own response to MSA which will probably vary from his predecessor.

"Person 3" enters the area and rendezvous with MSA. Once again there is no absolute moral truth for him to depend on for direction so he draws upon his own versions of experiences, intellect, environment, and opinions. Since these things probably differ from those of the first two, his conclusions about how to handle MSA will also differ to a certain extent.

Can you see the pattern here? Persons 4, 5, 6, 100, 1,000, up to "Person Last on Earth" all encounter the same moral situation. Since none of them have absolute truth to guide them in making their evaluations, they each use their own experiences, intellect, environment, and opinions, and whatever other tools are available to them. Their conclusions can be as varied as they are, and even if a couple of them resolve the moral question exactly the same, we still end up with a contradiction.

For each person who confronted this moral situation, the statement, "There is no absolute moral truth" was applied. Going back to our definition of an absolute truth, it is a truth that never changes and pertains to everyone equally. Concerning this MSA, the statement, "There is no absolute moral truth" did not change and was the only common guiding principle for all who met up with MSA. In other words, everyone who encountered Moral Situation A used the standard that there was no absolute moral truth to escort them in their decision-making, and the ideal of no absolute moral truth applied equally to everyone. So based on our definition we can conclude that the statement, "There is no absolute moral truth" is itself an absolute moral truth which makes the statement false. It disproves itself. How can absolute moral truth not exist when saying it doesn't is itself an absolute moral truth?

We said that each person meeting up with MSA used the faculties of their own personhood to guide them in their decision making. But that was only after the supposition that there was no absolute moral truth to rely upon. The statement, "There is no absolute moral truth" was the first guiding principle that each person used. Only after that did they employ the other methods of reasoning available to them.

It is impossible to say that absolute truth does not exist when that principle is utilized by everyone who encounters Moral Situation A. And it's not just this one particular moral question involved here. Moral Situations B, C, D, up to the last of all moral questions would all be resolved using the denial of absolute truth's existence if indeed no absolute truth existed.

If someone tries to counter by saying that maybe for this one person, or maybe for that one situation we won't apply the rejection of absolute truth, they are actually saying that absolute truth exists. The slightest deviation from the statement, "There is no absolute moral truth" opens up the possibility of absolute truth's existence. If we can't say that there is no absolute moral truth, then absolute moral truth must exist.

So what's the bottom line? Does this mean that there is a whole set of absolute moral truths that we have available to us in making our moral decisions? Actually that is not the case. What we have proven here is that there has to be at least ONE absolute moral truth and that is all. To deny that there is no absolute moral truth only proves that absolute moral truth exists. It doesn't prove how many truths, nor does it prove what qualities that absolute moral truth has, just that there has to be at least one.

So where do we go next. If an absolute moral truth exists, then what? The first question that comes to mind is who or what decided that this moral truth was absolute or even true in the first place? Truth is not truth unless there is a truth-giver. Obviously something had to authorize its absoluteness. What is that authority? Is it a person? Is it an entity of some kind? Is it "The Force" of Star Wars? Is it aliens who visited our planet centuries ago? Is it God?

Let's ask ourselves the following question. What

qualities would the authenticating power behind this absolute moral truth have? If this absolute moral truth is something that has never changed in the past, cannot now change in the present, nor can ever change in the future, then what characteristics would the one who gives the truth its absoluteness have? Let's look at a few of those.

Freedom from outside influences would seem to be a good trait for someone in that position. The source of absoluteness would have all the knowledge he needed to proclaim that this moral truth is absolute and would never need changing, and no other person outside of himself would have sufficient influence to cause a change of heart.

Neither would the source of absolute truth change his own opinion about something. He would have based his assertion of absoluteness after carefully considering all aspects of the matter. If he were to modify his beliefs then there would be a possibility of also modifying the absolute truth which, of course, would negate its absoluteness.

The source of absolute truth would need to be changeless, with no possibility of reconsidering his decision about the absolute moral truth he has established. The source of absolute moral truth would also have the power to enforce the truth. What good is truth if there are no consequences for failure to meet the requirements of the truth? There could be no thing or no one greater than the source who could nullify the consequences set forth by the source for disobedience.

Eternality is another essential ingredient for the source of absolute moral truth to have. The most radical change something could experience is from a state of non-existence to existence and vice versa. To have a beginning or an end would invalidate absoluteness.

As a Christian, I look at these characteristics of the source of absolute truth and conclude that God is that source and that there are many absolute truths, not just one. But that is a conclusion drawn from faith, not logic. We cannot absolutely prove the existence of God. We can't drive our car to an address such as 100 Heavenly Lane, look through a window of the house located there and expect to see God's throne. There are no road signs that say, "God – 15 miles ahead." If you typed the word "God" into your GPS, the female English voice would say, "You have got to be kidding, love." If we could prove the existence of God then where does the idea of faith come in?

While we can't logically prove that God exists, there are many things around us that point us in His direction. Nature screams to us that a Supreme Being exists. How can a person look at the order of this earth we live on and not wonder about the existence of God?

The Periodic Table is an example of the magnificently structured nature of our world. This table lists the basic elements that comprise all that exists. Right now there are 118 of them. Each element is assigned a number based on how many protons their respective atom has. For instance, Hydrogen has 1 proton therefore its atomic number is 1. Helium is number 2, Lithium number 3, and so on.

The amazing thing about these elements is the rock solid way in which they interact. When two number 1's (hydrogen) marry up with one number 8 (oxygen) the resulting material is water (H_2O). It is never anything else. Two hydrogen's plus one oxygen always produces water. One number 11 (sodium) combined with one number 17 (chlorine) gives us what we use to enhance the flavor of our food, salt (NaCl). This combination will not produce pepper or any other spice, only salt. How sweet it is to add together twelve number 6's (carbon), twenty-two number 1's (hydrogen), and eleven number 8's, (oxygen) and pour it on our cereal in the mornings. That's the formula for table sugar. And many of us just can't start the day without our eight number 6's (carbon), ten number 1's (hydrogen), four number 4's (nitrogen), and 2 number 8's (oxygen). That's the formula for caffeine. Every particular combination of these elements produces one, and only one particular result. There isn't the remotest chance that H2O would be anything but water. This scientific reliability does not prove God's existence, but it sure points us in His direction. To think that this kind of absolute molecular stability could happen by chance just doesn't make sense.

How about the issue of design? Nothing is built without some thought put into it. Everything necessary to erect a house could be spread out over an acre of land, from the plumbing fixtures to the electrical elements to the flooring, but no builder would dare drive the first nail unless he had a blueprint to work by.

The simplest thing that we as humans can build still requires a designer. When my youngest daughter was about kindergarten age, she took three pieces of wood of equal lengths, nailed them together in a "U" shape and gave it to me when I got home from work. She didn't just take some wood and nails, throw them up in the air and see what came down. The idea had to originate in her mind first, and then she had to figure out how to build it. There was probably some trial and error, but she had to utilize her brainpower to sort through the different ways it could be built. Nothing was done by happenstance. Her marvel of engineering is sitting by my computer today housing my unpaid bills awaiting their due dates. Even though she did not have a physical blueprint, still she designed that little implement in her mind as she built it.

If the most elementary of instruments requires a designer, does not nature with all the unbelievable intricacies also require someone to design it, someone with amazing abilities? Again, this does not prove God, but it sure sends us toward Him.

Witnessing the birth of a child advances our thoughts in God's direction. The miracle of the beginning of life is a moving experience that prods us to think about where that life came from. I still wonder at the awesomeness of my three children's births when I think of these little bundles of life that ten months earlier didn't even exist. Wow!

The testimony of a changed life points us in the direction of God. When we run into someone from our past who is totally different from the person we remember them as, and they tell us that God has changed their life, that should start us considering the reality of God.

How many other things nudge us in the direction of God? This chapter is one of them. The existence of absolute truth does not prove the reality of God, but it sure is hard to explain absolute truth apart from God.

When Jesus was talking with Nicodemus He equated those who are born of the Spirit with the wind. You can't see the wind, but you can see its effects on the treetops. You have no doubts that a chilling wind is blowing in the winter because your skin feels colder than the actual temperature. Wind is invisible yet there is not a person on earth that doesn't believe in its existence. Everyone concedes the reality of wind because of its effects, not its visibility.

Similarly, God is invisible. We can't see Him but there are tons of persuasive arguments of His existence surrounding us. Nature, life, intricacies of design, and myriads of other things lead us toward God, but do not provide physical or visible evidence of His existence.

Why doesn't God offer absolute proof of His existence? Why doesn't He open up the windows of

Heaven and Hell and give us a glimpse of their realities? I can't imagine anyone actually seeing Heaven's splendors and Hell's agonies who would choose the flames rather than the Light. But what would their motivation be? Would they be choosing Heaven because of the relationship they would have with God, or would they be exercising self-preservation and thinking about their own comfort, in effect using God instead of loving Him? Which motivation is the one that God wants a person to have for choosing Him?

Why is the existence of absolute truth on a personal level important? Why the fuss? Is absolute truth really significant in our daily lives? More than significant, it is essential for those of us trying to redirect our thinking away from the lies we grew up with. How many times did my mood change as I was growing up based on what others thought of me? Remember the story about my car with scripture stenciled all over it. One person making an off the cuff remark within my hearing changed how I felt about the car. I almost instantly went from loving that car to being ashamed of it and wanting to get rid of it at the earliest possible moment.

My entire life was an incredible roller coaster ride. If the emotional roller coaster I rode was an actual amusement park ride, it would be the biggest and fastest with the most ferocious twists and turns ever created. Whenever I heard or did something good I started an uphill climb. I remember participating in a spelling bee in my elementary school. This was the first leg of the national spelling bee that's held in Washington D. C. every year. I came in second which allowed me to proceed to the next step involving students from my entire school district, just two steps away from Washington. I came in fourth in the entire district. That finish wasn't good enough for me to continue, but the result of this experience is that I have always been a good speller. It's amazing how good experiences can propel you to a lifetime of achievement in a certain area.

As high as experiences like that took me, there weren't enough of them to counter the lows. I remember being chosen as a crossing guard in fifth grade. I was assigned to a certain corner and there was one kid who refused to listen to me. He berated me in front of the other kids saying that he didn't have to do what I said because he was in sixth grade and was only in fifth. I was too scared to stand up to him. I'd leave class a few minutes early each day to go to my assigned spot dreading the confrontation that was surely coming. Once that kid passed the rest of the afternoon went smoothly. I was just too meek and lowly to stand up to this bully, or even to tell the teacher in charge of our group what was happening. I just suffered through the entire year. Unfortunately, these kind of encounters propelled me to the downs of my roller coaster more often that the ups.

This is exactly why we need the absoluteness of God. Circumstances change. People change. How we are treated changes. If we base our self-worth on these things, we are destined for emotional earthquakes.

When God says something about us, we can be confident that His appraisal is true and unchangeable. He knows everything there is to know about us. He is not selective is His assessment. He doesn't own a pair of rose colored glasses. God does not have mood swings. He doesn't wake up on the wrong side of the throne on some mornings. Rainy Mondays are no different than sunny Saturdays. He never experiences Wednesday hump days. He is the epitome of consistency. What He thinks about you today is the same thing He thought about you yesterday, and it is what He will think about you tomorrow.

We need this anchor of unchangeableness in our lives. The world is just too unstable to rely upon, too many variables that can inflict upheaval. If the world's fickleness is what we trust in to ascertain our value then we will be greatly discouraged.

God has a clear picture of who we are and when He says that we are valuable enough to Him to send His only Son to this earth to take the punishment we deserve for our sins, we should pay attention. In Matthew 6 Jesus points out that even though the flowers growing in the field and the birds flying overhead don't do anything to earn their keep, God makes sure that they have everything they need. He says that we are of much more value to Him than the flowers or the birds.

Who can put a price on the value of the Son of God? If the entire earth was a diamond its worth would be inconsequential compared to the worth of God's Son. If the sun consisted of pure gold, a million suns would be worthy of nothing more than the trash heap when compared to the worthiness of the Son of God. If every ounce of matter in this universe was made of the most precious jewels, the Son of God's worth would reduce those jewels to dust. If any of these inestimable riches needed salvation, the Father would not have deemed them valuable enough to give His Son for them.

Yet when I was in need of just such a salvation, God willingly gave His Son for me. What does that say about how valuable I am to the Father? It must mean that I am pretty important to Him. This is an absolute truth. Contrary to the opinions of others that change based on all kinds of things, God's estimation of my worth to Him is unchangeable. So when I conclude that I am deeply loved, I will never have to alter that conclusion because the truth behind it, which is the value God has placed on me as a person, will never change. I can be confident.

I've spent the better part of my whole life with a fluctuating self-worth based on the "shifting sand foundations" of people's opinions, changing circumstances, personal accomplishments (or lack thereof), treatment at the hands of my fellow man, and a continual bombardment of data from all those things that the world deems to be important.

Now my goal is to direct my mind toward the "solid-rock foundations" of the truth of God. This is where I can find stability. This is where I can find certainty. This is where I can lose the fear of rejection. This is where I can exchange my vacillating self-image for one that is unbending in the face of the contradictory messages from the world around us. And so can you.

When God says that He loves you, take that to your emotional bank and deposit it with confidence. You will never have to withdraw even the smallest amount and it will reward you with the interest of peace and emotional well-being, compounded daily.

Absolute truth or relative truth: what is your spiritual house resting on?

CHAPTER 12

JUST LIKE A COMPUTER

You go to the store, pick out a new computer, take it home, and boot it up.

You go to the hospital, suffer through labor pains, take a new baby home, and start to raise it.

Your computer comes standard with an operating system, various and sundry programs, and storage space which is empty.

Your baby comes standard with hunger, thirst, various and sundry senses such as taste and smell, and a brain that is empty of experiences.

Your computer's storage space begins to fill up with files that you create. They could be documents, graphics, pictures, videos.

Your baby's brain begins to fill up with experiences you give to it. They could be the sights and sounds of household pets, the feel of new toys, the sensation of being tickled.

Your computer doesn't care about the content of what you are saving into its storage. A great literary work is the same as collection of redneck jokes. A picture of the Taj Mahal is no different than a photo of rover sleeping on the floor. The content of the material is immaterial to the computer. It just stores whatever is sent to its memory.

Your baby doesn't care about the content of the experiences being recorded in its brain. He can't distinguish whether the data he is receiving is good or bad. He can't decide to accept one experience and reject another. It is all the same him

But there is one judgment call that babies make about

every experience they encounter, and that is this. Everything is true.

God has programmed a child's brain to "autosave" memories every moment. From even before birth, while he is still in the womb, a child is soaking up everything he hears, sees, touches, smells, and tastes. Nothing escapes his notice. A child is ingesting information every moment about this new world he has been so rudely thrust into. And to a child, there is no good or bad, there is only true. He has no ability to reason. He has no ability to reject. He has no powers of deduction with which to debate the issues in his mind. He can only assume that all he takes in about his new world is accurate and trustworthy. He just accepts everything as true.

Perhaps this is why Jesus said in Luke 18:17, "Whosoever shall not receive the kingdom of God as a little child shall in no wise enter therein." A child just accepts what he learns as truth. So when God tells him that he needs a Savior, he is predisposed to agree and do what needs to be done. That's why God made such a big deal of parents instructing their children, "speaking of (these words of mine) when you sit in your house, when you walk by the way, when you lie down, and when you rise up" (Deuteronomy 11:18-19). Children who believe God's Word when they are young are more inclined to act upon their belief.

But here's something that I think gets lost. We generally talk about the five senses of hearing, seeing, touching, smelling, and tasting. But I submit that there is a sixth sense that should be included with the first five as an equal, and that is the sense of feel. Not the physical sense of touch, but the ethereal sense of feelings or emotions. A child experiences these just as surely, and possibly more acutely, than any of the others. He hasn't learned the art of suppression or the ability to analyze. He just feels.

A child stores everything he feels, whether it's happiness, sadness, contentment, uneasiness, confidence, guilt, love, indifference, an innumerable array of emotions are cached away for later recall. And their accuracy is unquestioned. The emotions he experiences absolutely and faithfully represent to the child the makeup of his new world. There is no doubt. The messages embedded in these feelings are never challenged.

The feelings generated inside the young child become the building blocks of his future emotional life. They could convey love, hope, encouragement, happiness, or they could communicate rejection, sorrow, discouragement, and sadness. As a child grows and the memories of the experiences which produced the building blocks vanish, the influence of the building blocks continues. All future experiences are constructed on top of these basic building blocks which were erected during the earliest years of existence.

Every construction expert will tell you that you had better pay a lot of attention to the foundation of a building. It needs to be laboriously level and square. Even a quarter of an inch variation can be fatal to the structure of a building. As you start building the second, third, or higher floors, the flaws in the foundation become noticeable. Each floor will accentuate to an increasingly greater degree the mistake made on the foundation.

We all have emotional foundations in our lives which were solidified early on. None of us collected all good messages, and none of us accumulated all bad ones. We all received varying percentages of both, some tilting toward the good, others tipping the scale toward the bad. Whatever combination built our foundation that was the groundwork upon which we erected the houses of our lives. If we have inputted more positive than negative information, then our house will be more solid. However, the more skewed our intake was toward the negative, the shakier will be the upper floors of our house as we get older.

But all is not lost. As we age, we can begin to assess the things we've learned based on new information. We are not forever cursed to endure the house of our lives and its foundational first floor. Houses can be redesigned. We can knock a wall down here, put a new door in there, repaint the walls, install new flooring, we can do any number of things to improve on what the original house looked like. Likewise, we are not condemned to a life sentence of unalterable thinking. We have the ability to knock down a thought here, open up a new way of responding there, change the color of our attitudes, or walk in a new belief system. Even our foundations are not immune from redesign. We can change our foundations. We can alter our beliefs about our world and about ourselves. We are not without hope.

If I had not engaged in Bible reading and study during my eighteen months of isolation, God could not have engineered the renewing of my mind that I so seriously needed. Make no mistake. It was God's work, not mine. Nothing I have done in my life would have been possible had God not used His Word in my life to produce changes in thinking.

The renewing of the mind. How does it happen?

CHAPTER 13

TRUTH REPLACEMENT

The biggest lie I faced was my faulty perception of the Heavenly Father. As I have said, to me God the Father was duty-driven, somewhat detached, only keeping His promises because that's what He was supposed to do. There was no desire, no emotion on His part in His relationship with me. I was a bit of a black sheep in His family. He saved me because He had to, simply because He said He would, so He was obligated.

More than that, the disparity between my response to praise and worship music versus some others around me was considerable. Oh, how I would stand there, wanting what they had, trying to manufacture the emotion inside of me that I was seeing in others, but never accomplishing the feat. It was extremely frustrating and discouraging. Why was I not allowed to experience God the way others seemed to be?

A major player that dogged me in this battle often was guilt.

Guilt separates us from God. Certainly, if that guilt is the result of an act of sin, then the guilt is real and confession is necessary to alleviate our guilt. In these cases, we understand why we feel guilty, we can account for our guilt as resulting from something we did wrong.

What about guilt that cannot be linked with an act of sin? I used to feel guilty a lot, yet I couldn't specify why. It was guilt without a cause, remorse without an origin, shame without a reason. I would just feel a vacuous, dulled, sense of personal abasement, a vague feeling of not living up to expectations. This is false guilt, when you feel guilty, but you are unable to establish a reason for the guilt.

Whether a guilty feeling is true, resulting from an act of sin, or false, having no apparent source, both have the same effect. Both separate us from God. True guilt as a matter of fact because we committed a sin. False guilt as a matter of perception. We may not be truly guilty before God, but a false sense of guilt just as surely erects a barrier between us and God as true guilt, except the barrier is of our own making.

My false guilt caused me to not want to approach God in prayer because I felt like I had somehow disappointed Him. I did not meet up to His expectations. I wasn't someone he really wanted to hear from because I just didn't measure up.

Of course, false guilt is a lie, a tool Satan uses quite effectively in some of our lives to paralyze us and keep us from the free and unhindered relationship with God that God wants us to have with Him.

In all of these things, I knew in my head what the Bible claimed to be true, but my experience contradicted the Bible. I knew that if I couldn't connect my guilt with a sinful action, that the guilt was false. I knew it, but I experienced the guilt anyway. What was in my head was not in my heart. How was I to bring my experience into unison with my head? What would it take to rectify this imbalance between what I knew and what I felt?

The foundation of my spiritual house was in need of major repair. When it came to my perception of God the Father, it was nowhere near square or level. There's a tourist attraction in Myrtle Beach, South Carolina and other places call Wonderworks. It's an upside down house and you walk through the house on the ceilings of the rooms. That's how badly the spiritual foundation of my house was constructed, and it needed to be redone if I was to have any semblance of fulfillment in my relationship with God. It was not an option. I had to rebuild. But how?

It required an alteration in how I thought.

God is duty-driven – that's a lie.
God has no emotion toward me – that's a lie.
I can never experience God like others do – that's a lie.
I am guilty, even though I don't know why – that's a lie.

These are all feelings that drove my lack of contentment with my relationship with God. Why did I have these feelings? Because I had believed these lies for so long that the truth seemed to have very little impact. The truth that I knew in my head was powerless against the lies that had permeated my thought processes for so long.

Somehow my belief system had to change. The truth had to replace the lies. But how?

Suppose you've been having problems with one of your knees. You're experiencing a certain level of pain, you're knee is not as mobile as it used to be, maybe you're even using a cane to help you get around. You're doctor sends you to an orthopedic surgeon who runs through all the tests and determines you need a knee replacement.

You have the surgery, but then comes the hard part – the therapy. Your new knee doesn't just automatically work. It's not like a new engine in your car. You need to restore strength and mobility to all the muscles and ligaments around your knee so they can perform as they should.

You suffer through quadriceps sets, straight leg raises, ankle pumps and a myriad of other tortures your physical therapist inflicts on you. If all goes right, you will eventually return to normal activities with no pain.

Suppose you've been having some problems emotionally. The negative thoughts are weighing on you and you're struggling to do the things you used to do easily. The path back to normalcy is similar to replacing a joint in your body. You have to first replace the thoughts, or lies, that are causing the problems with new thoughts that reflect the truth. Remember, the truth will set you free.

Then there are the exercises, mental exercises, to strengthen those truths until they become the ones dominating your thoughts and motivating your feelings and actions.

Three of the nastiest words in the English language are these – "it's a process." I wish that I could just snap my fingers, twitch my nose, fold my arms and blink like a television genie, and it would all change in an instant. Not gonna happen. It's a process, unfortunately. It takes time, it takes effort, it takes steadfastness, it takes honesty.

I call this process mental therapy. Unlike a knee that takes just a few hours to replace and a few weeks or months of therapy to strengthen, truly replacing the lies with the truth essentially requires a lifetime. It's an exercise of persistence with lots of setbacks and triumphs.

For me, this mental therapy has five steps to it. These steps are Recognition, Rejection, Replacement, Response, and Renewal.

RECOGNITION: Learning what lies we have been harboring.

2 Corinthians 10:5 encourages us to "…bring every thought into captivity to the obedience of Christ." What does it mean to bring something into captivity? In the case of a fugitive from the law, it requires a team of detectives and police officers searching through clues, following tips, doing legwork to finally catch the lawbreaker and bring him to justice. They don't just sit at the station drinking coffee,

and expect the fugitive to show up and surrender. They have to make the effort to corral their man.

Like the police, we must be active in our efforts to bring our fugitive thoughts into captivity. Thoughts that are dishonorable to God are fugitives from the obedience of Christ. They are spiritual outlaws, lies that run from the truth. They are holed up in the hideouts of our minds, fighting every advance truth tries to make on them.

My process of recognition began with the death of Dr. Jerry Falwell. As I have mentioned, I had made him a father figure. He was the kind of person who endeared himself to you without even trying. I placed him in a certain position of reverence in my life. I gave him prominence that I probably shouldn't have, but considering my background, it was understandably easy to do.

This adoration of Dr. Falwell effectively masked the issues I had with the character of God. They never surfaced because there was this buffer in my life that prevented these issues from arising. But when Dr. Falwell died, so did the buffer, and I was faced with all these questions about God that I hadn't dealt with before. I began feeling the stuff that had been hidden all these years, experiencing the negative impact untrue beliefs can have on a person. The frustration, anger, and bitterness, of feeling like a second class Christian invaded, and my faulty beliefs about God began taking their toll.

God used the death of Dr. Falwell to bring about the recognition in my life that I didn't really know who God was, and that became the focal point of my life. I had to recognize the times when my faulty view of God affected how I felt and behaved. I had to become a vigilante of my own life, constantly wary, constantly questioning, constantly assessing my thoughts. I had to scrutinize my feelings by determining the thoughts behind the feelings.

What did I believe that caused me to feel or act a certain way?

However, a word of warning. It's easy when doing these things to become paranoid. We can over analyze, sense things that aren't really there, create our own issues. It's a danger we must avoid because if we start trying to fix things that don't really exist, we can cause problems on top of the problems we already have. It's important to not manufacture what doesn't exist.

We must understand that we are not alone in this little exercise. We have a partner. We have a friend. We have someone whose job description it is to bring things like this to our attention. That person, of course, is the Holy Spirit. It's important to not get ahead of Him. He has our best interests at heart. It is His job to convict of sin, and that is ultimately what lies are. The lies that we may be believing are sinful in their nature, and it is the Holy Spirit's desire to bring these lies to their knees and knock them out of our lives.

When we start feeling something that we shouldn't, such as the guilt I explained at the beginning of this chapter, we should ask ourselves why we are feeling this way. It is at this point where we must be careful. We have to wait for the Holy Spirit to bring to our minds those thought processes that resulted in those feelings. It's His job, not ours. We are not required to come up with the answers. We are simply asked to allow the Holy Spirit to do His job and reveal to us the truth about ourselves and how we are thinking.

If nothing comes to mind at the time of the question, then don't panic, don't get frustrated, don't worry about not receiving the answer. It's okay. It's not the end of the world. Just stick it on the back burner of your mind and move on. The Holy Spirit will reveal the answer when you are ready for it.

The Holy Spirit is on your side in your struggles. He's not angry with you because of your questioning. In fact, He is honored that you are wanting to learn the truth about your faulty thinking. He is glorified with your desire to search for the truth. Don't ever think that the Holy Spirit is frustrated with you. He loves you and His primary concern is that you discover the lies that are causing your problems and continue the process to replace those lies with the truth.

We must question why we are feeling the way we do. We must seek to know and understand our thoughts and motivations with the intention of replacing them with right thoughts. We must ask God, the Holy Spirit, to reveal to us what thoughts are displeasing to Him and hurtful to us.

In the case of my guilt feelings, if nothing came to mind that could explain how I felt, then I had to assume that the feelings were the result of wayward thinking. At that point, it was time to move on to the next step of…

REJECTION. It's decision time.

This step is not very complicated. Now that the Holy Spirit has brought to our attention false beliefs in our thinking, we must declare our intentions with regard to these beliefs. Will we accept or reject them? Will we acknowledge that what we have been thinking is false, or will we continue to appease our misguided beliefs?

We are going to make a decision one way or another. Accepting false beliefs requires us to do nothing. By not deciding to challenge what we believe, we are actually making a decision to continue allowing those beliefs to dictate to us how we feel and how we'll act. No decision is a decision for the status quo.

We tend to be comfortable with what we are familiar with. The status quo is often a cozy place to be. It's safe, tame, risk-free. It's an intimate friend who has stuck with us for the long haul of our lives, and we are sometimes reluctant to give up the familiarity of our pal.

The longer we have languished in this place of stagnant belief, the harder it is to become free of its muck. So, even though our mental state may not be as positive as we would like, our tendency is to accept it and maybe hope that something will change. Sticking with what we know is sometimes less painful than trying to change. It's too easy to just be content with where we're at and not want to make the effort necessary to adapt our thought patterns to the truth.

That's why God sometimes has to tighten the screws just a little bit. He does not want us to be content with faulty thinking. He's dedicated to seeing truth take over our lives, so He takes our comfort zone and shrinks it until we can't fit in it any longer. He gradually constricts the number of places or situations where our lives are at least bearable, while increasing the places and situations that cause us consternation. Over time, there is a lessening of comfort and an intensifying of anxiety until we face up to what is causing our anxiety and decide to do something about it. He forces us into a position where we can't get comfortable enough.

It's better to make that decision early before the screws get tightened, but either way, after we reject, it's time to move on to...

REPLACEMENT. In other words, believe the truth.

Lies are screamers. They want all the attention we can give them. They want to dominate our thinking. They don't surrender just because we don't like them. They don't take hints. They only leave when we force them out by replacing them with truth.

There is an interesting story told by Jesus in Matthew

12, verses 43-45.

"When an unclean spirit goes out of a man, he goes through dry places, seeking rest, and finds none. 44 Then he says, 'I will return to my house from which I came.' And when he comes, he finds it empty, swept, and put in order. Then he goes and takes with him seven other spirits more wicked than himself, and they enter and dwell there; and the last state of that man is worse than the first."

This can correlate with what we are talking about here. It is not enough to just reject, we must replace as well. Rejection and replacement are blood brothers. Their execution in our process must happen one right after the other. If we don't replace the void left after we reject a lie, then the lie just comes back because it finds no resistance. Nothing has filled the space it just left and it returns to its home. Only when we fill the void left by the lie's departure with the truth, will the lie have a harder time reclaiming its old territory.

Focusing on the truth requires a certain level of mental forcefulness. The truth doesn't just take up residence, it must be invited into our minds, it must be welcomed.

There's an interesting element to when God called Moses to deliver His people from Egypt in Exodus 3:1-4.

"Now Moses was tending the flock of Jethro his father-in-law, the priest of Midian. And he led the flock to the back of the desert, and came to Horeb, the mountain of God. And the Angel of the Lord appeared to him in a flame of fire from the midst of a bush. So he looked, and behold, the bush was burning with fire, but the bush was not consumed. Then Moses said, 'I will now turn aside and see this great sight, why the bush does not burn.' So when the Lord saw that he turned aside to look, God called to him from the midst of the bush and said, 'Moses, Moses!'"

Moses was just taking a stroll on the mountain when he saw this unique sight, a burning bush that refused to give in to the fire. Moses made a decision to check it out. It was then that God began speaking to him.

Such is the case when it comes to us replacing lies with the truth. We must make the decision to turn toward the truth. When we turn, then God can begin speaking to us.

There are two aspects involved in replacing what we believe. They are study, and meditation.

In order to replace the lies with the truth, we need to know what the truth is. That means a study of God's Word because that is where we find truth.

When I felt like God was distant, uninterested, agitated with me, it's because those are the thoughts that dominated my thinking. I was simply experiencing the results of my belief system. It's what I had always thought, and so that's what I felt.

To find the truth, I looked to the Bible. Jesus said that whoever has seen Me has seen the Father. So I began by reading the Gospels exclusively for a year or more, paying particular attention to the character of Jesus, how He treated people, how He reacted to situations, just basically how He handled things. I wanted to know who God is. I wanted to understand His heart, His passions, who He is as a person. So as I read, I read with a purpose, looking specifically for those verses that showed me who God is.

That is still my purpose when I read the Bible today. I want to learn about the character of God, who He is, what He thinks, especially what He thinks about me. My main problem was a faulty understanding of my position with God. I felt uncared for and inferior. I felt condemned, unforgiven, unloved. I needed, and still need, a clearer understanding of who I am under God. It is a need I will have until I stand before Him and "know as I am known."

In regards to my guilt feelings, I had to understand that God's forgiveness is instantaneous. It is complete. It comes from a willing heart. God is someone who wants and desires to forgive. The verses describing the absolute forgiveness of God are many.

I John 1:9 – "If we confess our sins, He is faithful and just to forgive our sins and cleanse us from all unrighteousness."

Romans 8:1 – "There is now no condemnation for those who are in Christ Jesus."

Once I learned some of these truths, when the old way of thinking crept in, I told myself that that's not true, but this is, and thought of the Bible verses that revealed the character of God, which brings me to the second aspect of replacement – meditation.

We have to dwell on the truth as much as possible. I had spent a lifetime meditating on lies, now it was time to give truth a chance. Any time my mind wasn't preoccupied with something, I tried to focus on who the Bible says God is. Of course, much of the day is filled with things that require our attention, such as work and school, when we must concentrate our thoughts on the project at hand. We can go hours at a time without having a moment to think about God at all. He understands that. God certainly wants us to fulfill our responsibilities. But there will still be times when we have a breather for a minute or two. It is during these times when we can intentionally focus on God and the truth of His character. And it's important to make time every day, even for a few minutes, to deliberately meditate on the truth.

Many times we may feel the pangs of the lies of our past that try to bring us down, to clamp their claws into our thinking. It is then we need to again intentionally say "no" and deliberately focus on the truth. We may think, "God is getting tired of dealing with me." We must deny those thoughts and concentrate on the love of God as described in 1 Corinthians 13. Some of the elements of love listed are patience, kindness, not easily angered, does not keep a record of wrongs. We can apply all these to the character of God because God is love. 1 Corinthians 13 is a description of God. Philippians 4:8 implores us.

"Finally, brethren, whatsoever things are true, whatsoever things are honest, whatsoever things are just, whatsoever things are pure, whatsoever things are lovely, whatsoever things are of good report; if there be any virtue, and if there be any praise, think on these things."

Understanding the heart of God is the most effective way to deal with false guilt. The cross of Christ was completely sufficient. Nothing else needs to be added.

God has provided us with an amazing ability, and that is the gift of imagination – the ability to mentally visualize something that is probably not a reality yet. Children imagine friends that they can play with, or a future career as a fireman as they play with their fire engine. The boundaries are as limitless as our minds can conceive.

I have used my imagination in this process of replacement in the following way. Whenever I approach God in prayer, there are still feelings of not measuring up. My mind still wants to tell me that I am not who God says that I am, and I have to remind myself that what I am feeling is a lie. So, when I start to pray, the first word I say is "Father", and I then visualize myself as being part of a family. God's family. When I'm really feeling bad, I even imagine myself sitting on the lap of God and giving Him a hug. That's okay because that's how close God wants to be to us.

When I sense the lies, I use my imagination to visualize the truth. It reinforces the things that I have learned about the character of God, and helps protect my mind from the lies that want to reengage themselves in my thinking. When my natural self wants to regress to the old perception of God as distant and detached from me, I use my imagination to see God as He really is, a wonderful Father who loves me, holds me, and is intensely interested in every aspect of my daily life.

Imagination is one of the tools of replacement that God has given to us to help counteract the lies that would enslave us.

Once we meditate on the truth, then it is time for a…

RESPONSE. Acting on the truth.

This may be the most effective step in changing our beliefs, when we act on the truth.

During these times I would try my best to concentrate on the truth the God loved me, He had nothing against me, He was on my side. And then, I acted as if the truth was ruling the roost. Instead of walking around with a frown, barely acknowledging people I met, just going through the motions of my job, I tried to do just the opposite. It was hard at times.

Focusing on the truth requires a certain level of mental forcefulness. The truth doesn't just take up residence, it must be invited into our minds, it must be welcomed

Nothing changes our attitudes as much as ignoring the lies and acting on the truth. Instead of pouting and avoiding people, go ask someone if there's something you can do for them. Instead of moping around the house or office, go initiate some activity. Act like the truth is in charge of your attitude, no matter how much negativity you are feeling. Don't give in. Step out.

Many times I have felt like just staying where I was. I didn't want to do anything. I had no motivation because I was just feeling down on myself. I felt almost oppressed at times, shouldering a seeming physical burden that loaded me down on the chair I was sitting in. It was during these down times that I needed to get up out of the chair and take on the next task. I needed to reject the thoughts that were pinning me down, focus on the truth that God has freed me, and then act as if the truth was my motivation, even though I may have felt totally the opposite.

This is where faith comes in. We may sense nothing that remotely resembles the truth. We must believe the truth anyway. We may not be able to feel the slightest bit positive. Act positively anyway. We may feel like the lowest life form on earth. Act like you are a beloved, forgiven, child of the King anyway. Don't let the lies reign. Intentionally put the truth on the throne of your life. After you do this, then comes the…

RENEWAL. This is all God.

Romans 12:1 – "And do not be conformed to this world, but be transformed by the renewing of your mind, that you may prove what is that good and acceptable and perfect will of God."

The first four steps of this process involve at least some kind of action on our part. Recognize the lies, reject the lies, replace the lies with the truth, act on the truth. However, there is nothing that we can do that would accomplish the renewing of the mind. In fact, we are told to "be transformed", not to transform ourselves. Personal transformation is beyond our abilities.

Thank God for Strong's Concordance, from which I learned the following. The word used here in the original language is used three other times in the New Testament. Two of those are in the Gospels, Matthew and Mark, and refer to the time when Jesus "was transfigured" before Peter, James and John. The fourth is in 2 Corinthians 3:18, where it tells us that we "are changed", again, the action is performed upon us, not something we do ourselves.

God performs the renewing of our minds. And He does this because we have made the faith effort to believe truths instead of lies, and God rewards such endeavors with a fundamental change in our lives.

We may not consciously sense anything happening, but rest assured that God is at work.

CHAPTER 14

HONESTY

His anger against his brother had been festering for many long months now. Everything his brother did was golden. His own efforts, not so much. He was the elder of the two, and yet it seemed like whatever he did just never measured up to the standards set by his younger brother. The two discussed this situation many times, but a solution was elusive.

And so the anger, frustration, and jealousy, grew with each and every passing day until he had reached the breaking point. On that fateful day, he asked his brother to come with him out to the field where the crops were nearing the time for harvest. As they rehashed again the same old tired arguments, he noticed a deer at the edge of the field feeding on some of the plants. This was the diversion he was looking for. He directed his brother's attention to the hungry animal. When his brother turned away to look at the deer, he stooped down, picked up a rock from the ground, raised it high over his head, and crushed it into his brother's skull. His brother crumbled to the ground in a heap, blood rushing from the wound. His brother was dead.

With this, we have the first recorded sin in the Bible after the original sin in the Garden of Eden. Cain was angry about God's rejection of his sacrifice. Perhaps every time he saw his brother, Abel, he was reminded about his own shortcomings. Perhaps he thought that if he eliminated his brother, he would also eliminate the reminders. And so, the first murder was committed.

At this point, God intervened in a way amazingly

similar to what He did when He confronted Adam and Eve in the garden. He asked a question.

"Cain, where is your brother?"
"Am I my brother's keeper?" came the response.

Cain's answer to God's question was not exactly forthcoming. It was evasive and lacking information. God then responds to Cain with the truth which they both already knew. What Cain wouldn't admit it, God declared.

"What have you done? The voice of your brother's blood cries out to Me from the ground."

Having stated the truth, God then distributes the consequences of Cain's actions.

"Now you are cursed from the earth, which has opened its mouth to receive your brother's blood from your hand. When you till the ground, it shall no longer yield its strength to you. A fugitive and a vagabond you shall be on the earth."

I can imagine Cain cringing with each new revelation of punishment.

"You are cursed from the earth." Cain lowers his head.
"The ground shall no longer yield its strength to you." Cain slumps to his knees.
"A fugitive and vagabond you shall be on the earth." Cain falls face first to the ground.

He agonizes as he envisions a future life filled with frustration and loneliness. A life without hope. A life of

THE ISOLATION ROOM

constantly moving around from place to place, of struggling just to find enough food to eat. The torture he feels as he contemplates what his life will be like becomes unbearable and he blurts out his complaint to God.

"My punishment is greater than I can bear! Surely You have driven me out this day from the face of the ground; I shall be hidden from Your face; I shall be a fugitive and a vagabond on the earth, and it will happen that anyone who finds me will kill me."

If I had been God at this point, my response would have been something like, "So what? Cain, you are in no position to negotiate. You just committed the worst sin there is. You killed a man. Why should I care what you think?"

Fortunately, I guess, I am not God because God's reply to Cain's complaint was nothing like what mine would have been. God showed a certain level of compassion by setting a mark on him and promising vengeance on anyone who would kill Cain.

Why did God respond to Cain in this way? Why should He show any kind of compassion at all on someone who had just murdered his brother?

I think the answer can be found in Cain's response to God's punishment.

When God asked Cain about what he had done, Cain answered with evasiveness. "Who, me? Am I supposed to know everything my brother is doing?"

After God announced the consequences of what he had done, Cain responded with an outburst of honesty. "I can't take it. That's too much for me to bear."

To God's initial question, Cain was ambiguous. To God's pronouncing of punishment, Cain was honest.

When God asks a question, He is not looking for information, He is looking for honesty. I think that is why God showed a level of compassion toward Cain because Cain had ended up being honest with God.

Honesty is a huge deal. It is a requirement in our dealings with God. Obviously, we can't hide anything from Him. He is, after all, omniscient. He knows everything before it even happens. So, He doesn't need our enlightenment about particular situations. He is looking for our agreement.

That's what God has always wanted from us since the fall in Genesis 3. Our agreement that we are sinners. Our agreement that we need a Savior. Our agreement that Jesus Christ is the only way to Heaven. Only after we agree with Him on these things can He then deal with us on the question of submission to His solution to our sin problem.

When we are honest with Him and with ourselves, then He is able to deal with the struggles and situations of our lives. If we remain dishonest and won't admit things that are present in our lives, then we in essence handcuff Him by not allowing Him to handle things as they really are. God is seeking to impact the real issues of our lives, not the masks we put on. What good does it do for a fireman to aim his hose across the street from the house that's burning?

As someone who spent his life suppressing emotions, I was an expert in the area of dishonesty. It was my lifestyle. I never allowed myself to be honest when it came to my feelings. I lived as if a bunch of lies was the truth. Emotions didn't exist – a lie. They were a nuisance – a lie. They didn't do me any good – a lie. I was very skillful in the area of lying to myself. It was an art I had perfected. No one could deceive me like I could.

God's business with me centered on my accepting that

I had emotions that were both healthy and necessary for a fulfilling life. Until I became honest, He was not able to penetrate to the real issues of how I felt about myself and Him. He could not impart to me His real character until I admitted how I saw Him. He couldn't tell me about His passion and love for me until I accepted the misconception I had that He was a duty driven God with no desire toward me whatsoever.

Honesty is the great cleanser. It takes a certain effort to be dishonest. Dishonesty requires a suppressing of the truth and replacing it with a mindset of our own making. Honesty requires nothing but acceptance. Honesty flows. Dishonesty is a dam that redirects the flow. Honesty is as natural as the sun rising and setting each day. Dishonesty is as unnatural as men flying into space.

In order to overcome my misconceptions about God, I had to first become honest about my misconceptions about God. It was hard for a while. How could I admit that I was angry at God because I felt like a second class Christian when others could worship Him in a way I couldn't? How could I admit that I felt distant from God? How could I admit that I felt unloved by God? No good Christian should ever permit themselves to disclose such awful admissions, right? All these things I knew in my head to be false. Therefore, to admit how I felt was to fly in the face of God's truth. If the Bible declared something to be the truth, then for me to admit anything otherwise would be to dishonor God and reveal an unbelieving heart.

God had to get me to be honest before He could instill truth in me. As long as I was denying how I honestly felt, then God wasn't able to counter with the truth about His true character. Truth is always a victor over lies, but it can do nothing if lies are not admitted. Until I conceded how I felt, there was nothing for the truth to battle against.

I needed to understand that God already knew how I felt about Him. It came as no surprise. God's initial job, then, was to get me to be honest. Like Cain, and Adam and Eve before Him, God's dealing with me was not to gather information, it was to induce honesty. It was to bring me to the point of accepting myself as I really was, not as I thought I should be as a Christian. A Christian should never be angry at God. A Christian should never feel distant from God. A Christian should never feel like God doesn't care about them. To admit otherwise means to thumb our noses at the truth as revealed in the Bible. But God can't deal with sin until we admit that we have sin. Only then can He wield the sharp sword of His Word directly at the issue at hand.

In reality, my efforts to hide what I was truly feeling and replacing them with what I thought I should have been feeling as a Christian was nothing more than me trying to live the Christian life on my own. I was trying to manufacture holiness in my life. I was trying to put up a Christian front, not necessarily to others, but to myself. I couldn't admit my failures or shortcomings, otherwise known as sin. I was hiding myself from myself, which put up a roadblock against the truth that God wanted to teach me. I wasn't dying to myself, I was attempting to wrap myself in holy aluminum foil so that I could look all shiny. But that doesn't cut it with God. He wants honesty. Honesty is a prerequisite to holiness.

During this time in my life, if you asked me to confess a sin, any sin, I couldn't. That's because I wasn't honest with myself. I had erected such a hard shell around me that no one could get in, and I couldn't get out. To acknowledge even the slightest flaw in my character was impossible. I couldn't see my sin because I didn't let myself see it. This is how bad my dishonesty had distorted my perception of myself.

I had to concede my failure to truly understand the character of God. I had to accept myself as I really was, not as I wanted to be. I had to be brutally honest with myself, and therefore with God, before God could minister truth into my life.

For God to change us, He starts with who we are, not who we present ourselves to be. We must permit ourselves to admit the worst in us. Maybe that means we call God unkind or unfair. If that's how we truly feel, then we must be honest and make those accusations.

But as we relate to God how we really feel, there must be another aspect to our introspections. We must also recognize that what we are feeling and telling God about are lies. They are not who God really is, but only how we feel who God is. When we tell God honestly how we feel, in the back of our minds there needs to be a recognition that what we are feeling is not the truth.

"God, I know you are kind and no respecter of persons, but right now I feel like I don't amount to much in Your eyes."

"God, I know you are always with me, but I'm feeling all alone, like You are at the far reaches of the galaxy, totally unconcerned about me."

"God, I know you love me, but I feel like You just don't. I am a nuisance to You. I am a burr in Your side that You would like to get rid of."

We must recognize that what we feel does not reflect the reality of who God is. But before we can be endued with the truth, we must be honest about the lies. If we remain dishonest about how we feel about God, then we limit Him in what He can do in our lives.

Truth about lies is a necessity of life, even if that truth reveals the kind of sinful, nasty, disgusting person we are. God already knows. He is simply trying to get us to admit it. Then He can change us.

CHAPTER 15

ANGER: IT'S OK

I can't count the number of times I was frustrated because I wasn't experiencing the kind of relationship with God that other Christians seemed to have. I felt like a second class Christian, like God was favoring others over me, like I just didn't measure up. If you asked me if God loved me, of course I would have said yes. That's how a good Christian should respond. Did I believe it? More or less. Did I experience it? Not really.

I would get so frustrated at times that, after checking to see if anyone could see or hear me, I'd start screaming. "WHY CAN'T I HAVE WHAT OTHER CHRISTIANS HAVE? WHAT'S WRONG WITH ME? I AM TIRED OF BEING LEFT OUT. I'M TIRED OF FAKING IT. I WANT REALITY. I WANT TO FEEL IT. I WANT TO KNOW IT." I was usually driving down the road during these times, careful to have a safe distance between me and other vehicles. I'm sure if someone saw me, they would have called the men in white coats to take me away in a straitjacket.

I remember having one of these episodes as I was traveling to the first appointment with the last counselor I ever saw. I was just mad! I was furious because it just wasn't working for me. I hated not experiencing what others seemed to enjoy. Sometime during the session I mentioned about my anger on the way over, expecting a concerned response followed by a probing to find out why I behaved so strangely. This was obviously questionable behavior, right?

Instead, he leaned forward in his chair, cracked a smile, raised his fist, and said enthusiastically, "Good!" Not quite what I expected, but it made me think that maybe I was in the right place.

It's okay to get mad sometimes about the right things.

Often, I'd be in church during praise and worship, battling the thoughts of inferiority that were overshadowing my desire to join in praising God. Of course, I wouldn't scream or yell out loud, but in my head there was some major hollerin' going on, pretty much along the same lines as when I was in a car.

In fact, there were occasions when I would embody my battles. By that I mean that the feelings I was experiencing would be directed to a person in my mind. It would have arms and legs, but no face. It was not anyone in particular that I was envisioning, but rather a faceless creature that became the personification of all that I was wrestling with. It was my enemy, my attacker, the assailant of my soul, even bordering on being Satan himself. I would get so mad that, in my mind, I'd grab this creature by its body and with all the strength I could summon, I'd smash its head into one of the pews, preferably one of the sharp corners of the seats. I'd do it again, and again, and again. Then I'd stomp on its head, twisting my foot back and forth, grinding it into the carpet covered cement floor. I was merciless, relentless, pitiless, not stopping until I felt like I had made my point. I hated that person.

Of course, all this was in my mind's eye. No one around me could tell what was going on inside my head. To my knowledge, no one ever knew about these escapades into this world of anger, that is until I told my counselor about them. His response surprised me, and told me that I wasn't crazy.

James 1:20 says that the anger of man does not achieve

the righteousness of God (NASB). This was after James exhorted us to be slow to anger in verse 19. So the anger I was expressing was not accomplishing anything in the way of actually overcoming my feelings of inferiority.

So, why did my counselor consider these episodes good? If I was driving and saw someone doing what I was doing, I might call 911, afraid of what mayhem that driver might create. What did my counselor mean when he reacted so positively to my fits of anger?

The first chapter of the book of Judges gives us an insight. To me, the deliverance and subsequent taking of the Promised Land by the Israelites is a type of the Christian life. I can see so many parallels between the two, and we can learn from the successes and failures of the children of Israel during this time. Here is the litany in Judges 1:27-35.

"At that time Manasseh failed to drive out the inhabitants of Beth-shean, Taanach, Dor, Ibleam, and Megiddo, or any of their villages; for the Canaanites were determined to dwell in this land. When Israel became stronger, they pressed the Canaanites into forced labor, but they never drove them out completely. Ephraim also failed to drive out the Canaanites living in Gezer; so the Canaanites continued to dwell among them in Gezer. Zebulun failed to drive out the inhabitants of Kitron and Nahalol; so the Canaanites lived among them and served as forced laborers. Asher failed to drive out the inhabitants of Acco, Sidon, Ahlab, Achzib, Helbah, Aphik, and Rehob. So the Asherites lived among the Canaanite inhabitants of the land, because they did not drive them out. Naphtali failed to drive out the inhabitants of Beth-shemesh and Beth-anath. So the Naphtalites also lived among the Canaanite inhabitants of the land, but the inhabitants of

Beth-shemesh and Beth-anath served them as forced laborers."

Here we see that while the children of Israel took possession of their Promised Land, they didn't complete the task. God's command was for them to totally annihilate the inhabitants of the land.

"However, in the cities of the nations the Lord your God is giving you as an inheritance, do not leave alive anything that breathes. Completely destroy them—the Hittites, Amorites, Canaanites, Perizzites, Hivites and Jebusites—as the Lord your God has commanded you. Otherwise, they will teach you to follow all the detestable things they do in worshiping their gods, and you will sin against the Lord your God." (Deuteronomy 20:16-18).

Here, we see God telling the children of Israel to totally wipe out the cities of the Promised Land, including all who breathe. That's pretty inclusive. The reason being that any who are left will draw them away from complete devotion to God. God wanted the Israelites to experience His full blessing in the land, and He knew that any remnants from the previous societies would cause an erosion of that blessing.

Unfortunately, this is exactly what happened. Even though initially, the conquered people were relegated to forced labor, as time went on, their pagan practices began mixing with the pure Jewish practices and the worship of God became corrupted. Eventually, the worship the children of Israel offered became as bad as their predecessors, so God eventually expelled the Israelites – but not until they had multiple opportunities to repent.

The book of Judges recounts a dozen times when the Israelites strayed from their purpose in the land. Each time, God allowed some sort of oppression to inflict His people. The people turned back toward God, whereupon God provided a judge to deliver them from the oppression, and during the life of that judge, the people maintained at least some semblance of holiness.

Time and time again, 12 times to be exact, the Jews followed this same path. They worshiped God correctly, they slowly abandoned that worship, they were oppressed in some way, they cried out to God, God delivered them. Then the cycle repeated.

This cycle parallels my Christian life in this way. I will go through a period of relative peace where I am intentionally seeking after God. I get comfortable. Slowly, the lack of internal conflict, the absence of a crisis, will cause me to, almost imperceptibly, not seek after God with the same kind of desire as before. This happens in very small increments, so that I really don't notice it happening. God will then allow something to occur in my life that ramps up the pressure. Perhaps it stirs up lies of the past, or reveals a shortcoming in my life that needs to be corrected. I will become uncomfortable. I will start calling on God with more fervor to work in my life and take whatever it is away and replace it with His truth, (Make me comfortable again). God will faithfully perform that miracle in my life, thus restoring the relative period of peace that I started with.

It's just a fact of our human lives. We are lovers of comfort. We hate to hurt. We hate to be anxious. We hate insecurity. When these things happen in our lives, we'll do just about anything to get back to that place of peace. Some try to get there through drugs, sex, material things, whatever it is that they think will bring them to the point of experiencing peace.

The bottom line is that God wants the same thing for our lives, but He is the only One who can give us that peace. No thing or activity can take the place of God Himself. When God sees something in our lives that is blocking that peace, He will take action.

When we became Christians, in essence, we entered our own Promised Land. We were given what we didn't deserve and didn't work for.

God chose to give the Jewish people the Promised Land.

God chose to give us eternal life through the sacrifice of His Son, Jesus.

But, just as the Jews had to show their commitment to God by obeying the command to completely destroy the old inhabitants of the land, we also have commands to obey.

"Bring every thought into the captivity of Christ." (2 Corinthians 10:5)

"Whatever is true, honest, just, pure, lovely, of good report, think on these things." (Philippians 4:8)

"Don't be conformed to this world, but be transformed by the renewing of your mind." (Romans 12:10)

Just like the Jews of old, we have entered the Promised Land, but there's still work to be done. God wants all the old possessors of our lives to be completely eradicated. There is no place for old habits, old ways of thinking, old lies. We are new creations and the old should find no resting place in us.

But when things are going good, when God is blessing us, when there are no battles to fight, we tend to become complacent. We start to relax. We don't' have that edge about us the urges us toward a deeper relationship with God. The pursuit of holiness just isn't as urgent as when we are going through tough times.

This may not be intentional, it's just the way we are wired as human beings. Too many times, we need a jump-start. We need a boost. We need a nudge on the south end going north.

So, when I expressed my anger issues to my counselor and he reacted so positively, he was encouraging my determination to overcome the issues I was facing. My anger showed a certain spunk in that I was not happy with who I was and that I wanted to see change.

Certainly, if my anger had resulted in injury to someone or something, that would have been going too far. Ephesians 4:26 says "be angry and sin not."

It's okay to be angry at what is hurting you. God is. God hates the things in our lives that keep us from experiencing His full blessing. God hates the sins of our past that keep injecting their venom into our present lives. God hates the lies of our past that hold us back from relishing in His truth. God hates the past experiences of our lives that just won't let go, that continue to inflict pain on us today. God hates anything that gets in the way of His relationship with us.

So should we! But our tendency is to ignore what doesn't affect us at the moment. The Jews brought the old inhabitants of the land into subjection, or so they thought. They learned to live with the old instead of eradicating it. They thought they couldn't get hurt. How wrong they were. The old just slowly crept in, unnoticed, little by little, edging its way into their lives until the difference between the old and the new was negligible.

God then had to intervene in the Promised Land of

Israel, just as He does today in the Promised Land of our lives, to bring us back. He has to allow a little pressure to show us that we have strayed away, that we need to refocus. He needs to show us that we cannot live compatibly with the lies of our past. They must be obliterated. They must be treated unmercifully. They must be regarded as mortal enemies. They want to destroy us. We must destroy them first. With God's help we can, we must. A good dose of anger reveals just how much we want to defeat these enemies of our lives.

CHAPTER 16

WORSHIP

Nothing makes an adult act like an idiot more than a baby. I have three children and three grandchildren. The moment they were born I started coochie-cooing, making strange sounds, contorting my face, generally acting like an alien of myself. My goal? To get that first smile, that first curling of the mouth, indicating that the child was responding to me. It brought a real sense of joy to realize that this little life who was so young actually reacted to something I was doing. No matter how long it may have taken, I was going to do whatever was necessary to get that response.

Do you think God might be looking for the same thing from us? He has sent His Son to die for us. He has given us eternal life. He continues to bless us daily, even when we don't deserve it. God does and has done all these things for us. Doesn't it seem reasonable that God wants from us the same thing I always wanted from my newborn children and grandchildren – a response?

When we worship, aren't we giving God that little baby smile indicating our response to Him? Don't you think that it brings joy to His heart when His children acknowledge Him and His presence in their lives?

Worship is our little baby smile responding to who God is and what He has done in our lives.

"Who Mourns For Adonais?" That's one of the episodes from my favorite TV show of the 1960's, Star Trek. There's a lot of theology you can glean from that series, most of it bad, including from this episode.

The story line goes like this. The Enterprise is orbiting around the planet Pollux IV doing routine surveying of the planet's surface. They read no signs of life on the planet, and are stunned when the ship is grabbed by a giant hand and stopped dead in space. No amount of engine thrust can extricate them from the hand's grip. Then the source of the hand appears to them on their screen and invites them to the surface.

When they arrive they meet a man dressed in the clothes of earth's ancient Greek civilization, complete with a laurel wreath on his head. As the story goes, this man is one of a number of aliens with extraordinary powers who visited earth around the time of ancient Greece. They were immediately worshiped as gods, temples were built, and the memoirs of their exploits were published.

As time went on, the humans steadily outgrew the need to worship these beings and began drifting away to the point of ignoring them. The gods left, finally settling on the planet Pollux IV. Their hopes were that the human race would one day explore beyond the confines of Earth and reach their planet.

After many centuries most of the "gods" gave up waiting and spread themselves out before the wind, and faded away, all except this one. He introduced himself to the Enterprise crew as Apollo, the last of the Greek gods.

Here's where the bad theology starts. Apollo's desire was to love and meet the needs of these humans in exchange for their worship. He wanted them to begin a new civilization of humanity on this planet. He wanted to be their god and the crew to be his children.

But Apollo had a bit of a temper. He restrained himself for a short while, seemingly understanding that the humans needed time to adjust to this new reality. It wasn't long, though, when the crew of the Enterprise showed no signs of accepting their new situation, that Apollo began teaching some lessons.

Apollo wanted free-will worship from Captain Kirk and the crew. Instead he got resistance and downright disobedience. He got defiance instead of deference, dishonor instead of devotion.

Apollo began demonstrating his superior powers and demanding worship from the humans. If he couldn't get what he wanted with kindness, he'd get it with dominance instead.

By the end of the episode the humans had destroyed Apollo's power source. Apollo was rejected and ultimately reached the same conclusion that his compadres previously had, that humanity had outgrown their need for him. He faded away as the others before him.

The question I ask is this. How different is our God from the god Apollo of Star Trek?

To answer that question, let's revisit the last day of Creation and allow ourselves the luxury of a little sanctified imagination as we spy on God's activities.

It's about noon on Creation week's sixth day and the lunch whistle has just sounded. God sits down under one of His trees and opens the brown bag He packed that morning containing a turkey sandwich, chips, and a soda. He had spent the morning creating all kinds of animals, from the smallest of insects to the huge behemoths.

As he relaxes and munches on His lunch, some members of His creation saunter by His tree and God considers each one as they pass. First to wander through is a two-legged bird with a long tail of feathers twice the length of his body dragging the ground behind him. He raises himself up and spreads out his tail revealing a beautiful display of brilliant green and blue colors, like a hundred eyes peering back at God. God applauds the wonderful display. The bird ignores the adulation, closes its tail, and continues walking.

Next to arrive is a massive, slow moving fellow with big ears, a long hose-like protuberance from the font of his face, and two white tusks extending to points on each side of the hose. But God has to chuckle when the creature passes and the thin little tail comes into view, looking a little out of place on the big body. God wonders what possessed Him to punctuate this mighty beast with such a small exclamation point. He mentions this, but the creature just continues its journey as if he never heard.

Following closely is one of the behemoths standing upright on two thunder-inducing legs. Each step sends tremors along the ground. Everything gives this creature a wide clearance because when it turns, its massive tail threatens destruction to anything in its path. The trees shake in their roots at the sight of its teeth, for one good bite will leave little stubs where magnificent branches once regaled. Again, God chuckles to Himself as He eyes the two little arms looking even more lost and insignificant than the tail of the previous creature. And once again, God's expression of these thoughts to the brute meet with the same indifference as that of the other creatures. The behemoth thunders away.

A yellow bird flutters in for a landing a few feet from where God is sitting. It belts out a marvelous melody as loud as its little lungs will allow. God smiles. When its song is finished, God compliments the little musician on the beauty of what He had just heard. The little bird just flies off to its next concert, not acknowledging the appreciation of the audience it just left.

Other creatures large and small, fast and slow, flying and crawling, pass the God Who created them, each in their own way ignore every attempt God makes to communicate with them.

God's deliberates over what He has experienced while eating His lunch. He considers that none of His creation responded to His overtures. Every one of them ignored His attempts to interact with them. While God loved all of His creation, He realized that not one of them knew it. They could not acknowledge the love God had for them because they could not understand Him and how much He loved them, and this presented a challenge. What kind of being could God create that would have the capacity to acknowledge, understand, receive, and respond to the love God has for them?

When the whistle blows signaling the time to return to work, God knows what He must do. He rises up and scoops some ground into His hands. Nothing fancy, just a handful of normal, ordinary, everyday dirt. He begins to lovingly caress the shapeless mass into a form. With painstaking attention to detail, He crafts a body unlike any of the others He had created. He apportions it with precise accuracy, aligning with the vision God has intended for it. When He finishes, He surveys His creation and sees that it is good – to a point.

The body laying before Him is perfect in every way except for one thing. It has no life. God had given life to thousands of creatures over the course of six days, but it was life that could not recognize who He was or respond to His expressions of love toward them. He determines that this life has to be different from all the rest. More of the same is not enough.

What God does next shakes the entire universe, reverberating through every star, every solar system, every galaxy, and beyond. In the most marvelous and unexplainable act of selflessness, God kneels down beside the body He had just created, places His mouth over the nose, and breathes Himself into it. He literally shares His own being, His consciousness, His emotions, His desires, His love, causing the newly created life in this body to be the exact image of God Himself. To God, sharing His life with this new creation is an act of the deepest meaning, the innermost significance, the profoundest joy, an undertaking that overshadows everything He had done previously during the six days of creation.

As this new creation opens its eyes, the first thing it sees is the face of God, smiling. The first thing it hears is the voice of God, saying, "Hello, my child."

The above scenario was generated in response to a question I was once asked. The question was this. If God knows who will accept Him and who will not, why does He allow someone who He knows will end up in Hell to be born in the first place? Doesn't that seem rather cruel? If God knows that a child who is being born will spend his entire life never coming into a relationship with Him and end up in eternal agony, why doesn't God just not allow the conception of that child to happen? It would seem kinder to never be born than to leave the womb, live a life without God on this earth, and then experience an eternity of suffering without God.

That's a tough question, but let's take it a step further and include the entire human race. God knew when He created Adam, that Adam would sin and cause all kinds of heartache and suffering that God never intended for His creation to experience. God knew all about Genesis 3 before He ever formed Adam from the ground. He knew the tactics the serpent would use to lure His beloved ones away. He knew the ones who had received God's very own life would reject Him.

But even more astounding than all that, God knew

what it would cost Him! Did you get that? God knew full well what it would cost Him personally. God understood the price tag that accompanied the act of creating this creature in His own image. The Bible says that Jesus Christ was slain from the foundation of the world, (Revelation 13:8). God knew! He was not blindsided. There was no guesswork on His part. The path before Him was clearly marked in His own mind. God knew when He created Adam that Adam would stray away, and that the only way to get him back would cost the life of His own Son.

If I knew that something was going to cause my family to suffer, I'd do anything to avoid it. But God didn't avoid it. He embraced it.

This just makes the creation of man that much more astounding. God knew that creating Adam, a creature in His own image, would cost Him dearly. His only Son would have to give His life as a ransom of redemption. It was absolutely necessary. Otherwise, neither Adam, nor any of his descendants had the remotest chance of enjoying the fellowship with God that God intended for them to have.

What does this say about the character of God, that God would do something like this? What motivated God to weigh the costs of, against the desire for, designing a being who could respond to Him? Why did He want so much to have fellowship with a member of His creation that He would follow through with the creation of Adam, knowing full well that in doing so, He would have to sacrifice the life of His only Son? Why would God do this? What kind of love does something like this? What kind of love accepts the suffering in return for the fellowship, even if it's only with those image-bearers who willingly choose to accept the sacrifice of love on the cross, while the rest are relegated to an eternity of suffering without hope?

This act of God just astounds me. It's hard to

comprehend. He could have avoided the agony of the cross by simply not creating man in the first place. In my mind, this would have simplified things so much for God. No sin, no suffering, no cross. So what motivated God to accept the consequences the creation of man inflicted on Him?

I have tried in vain to understand the thought processes going on in God's mind when He created Adam. It's beyond my ability to comprehend, and the sense I get from God is, just accept it. Don't try to understand, just accept and be thankful for the love I have bestowed on you. But that doesn't make the selfless act of Adam's creation any less amazing.

This brings up another question. Since God created the human race so that we could respond to Him in worship, why? Why do we worship our God? What is the purpose of worship? Or even more important, why does God command us to worship Him? What is His motivation for wanting the worship of man? Do we fulfill some need God has? Does God have a human shaped hole in His being that our worship fills? Why does God want us to worship Him?

Let's give our sanctified imagination a little more work. Let's imagine God seated on His throne in Heaven listening to the prayers of His children on earth. There's one now, sending praises to the Father, and God is listening. Would the conversation go something like this?

Child of God: "Your power in creating the universe is beyond compare."

God: "Well, that's true. You haven't seen anyone else do it, have you?"

Child of God: "The love you showed on the cross is beyond understanding."

God: "Yeah, don't you know it."

THE ISOLATION ROOM

Child of God: "The beauty of your holiness is beyond comprehension."

God (a little distracted): "Oh, I'm sorry. Did you say something. I was just admiring my beauty."

Child of God: "Who can stand before Your great and awesome power?"

God (stifling a yawn): "Well, you're stating the obvious, aren't you. Everybody knows that."

Does God get bored with our worship? Of course, He knows who He is. He has complete understanding of His own character, His power, His actions. He doesn't need us to remind Him of who He is.

Does God need our worship? That would imply that before the creation of man, God had a need. He was somehow incomplete as a person and required something outside of Himself to fill that need.

Is God a narcissist? Does He have a vain streak in His character that needs massaging?

Is God lacking anything? Does he Have a self-image deficiency that hungers for approval or confirmation?

The answer to all of the above is a resounding, "NO". Then why does God want the human race to worship Him? What's the purpose? Who benefits from the worship of God? If not God, then who?

The only other entity involved in worship is us. If God doesn't need our worship, if worship doesn't benefit Him in some tangible way, then the beneficiaries of worship must be us. We are the ones who need worship. We are the ones profited by the experience of worship. God's ultimate goal for worship is to benefit us.

Isn't all that consistent with who God is? God shared Himself when He breathed life into the body of dirt, thus creating the human race. God shared Himself when Jesus was born in Bethlehem, relinquishing many of the perks of being God so that He could share Himself with humans as a human. God shared Himself on the cross, sharing His righteousness with us so that we could become children of God.

God's desire for us to know Him is a dominant theme in the Bible. He has revealed Himself to us in so many ways.

The existence of the Bible itself shows us that God wants us to know Him.

When John was on the Isle of Patmos, God met him and gave him and us the "Revelation of Jesus Christ."

In Psalm 34:8 we read, "O, taste and see that the Lord is good."

God's desire has always been for us to know Him, understand Him, love Him, worship Him. When we worship, as Darth Vader would say, we are fulfilling our destiny. God created us to know Him, fellowship with Him.

Does God have a need for worship? No, we do.

Does God have an issue with self-image? No, we do.

Does God need to be reminded of His attributes. No, we need the reminding, not Him.

Does God have a vain streak that requires massaging? No, we do, and worship takes our eyes off of our own vanity and focuses them on the God who humbled Himself on the cross.

God doesn't want our worship for His sake, He wants it for our sakes, so He can once again share Himself with us. When we worship, we give God the opportunity to show us who He is, how much He loves us, how much He has done for us.

Every time we worship, we are opening ourselves up to understand God a little bit more.

Every time we worship, we allow God to once again share Himself with us.

If we have a problem with self-image, and mine was supremely negative, we open up the chance for God to share just how much we mean to Him. We are reminded that He sent His Son to die for us, that His thoughts toward us are only positive, wanting only what's best for us. When we get down on ourselves, worship will help us realize just who we are in Christ, that God is on our side, that we are so valuable to Him that He created us knowing full well what that act would cost Him. We are reminded that God wants us, cares for us deeply, is faithful to bless us. This kind of knowledge, as we meditate on it, will eat away at the negativity in our lives and replace it with truth that builds up.

CHAPTER 17

RAINDROPS

It's a dreary day outside as I sit here in my living room. The incessant pounding on my skylight and a quick look out the window testify to the fact that thousands of raindrops are falling from the sky every second.

Each raindrop, as it falls, lands on some kind of surface. It could be water such as in a pond or river, it could be soil, rock, any number of surfaces on our planet are receptors of each raindrop.

If a drop lands in water, it is immediately assimilated and becomes one with its new acquaintance.

If it lands on soil, it is absorbed with varying speeds depending on the ground's dryness. Its moisture is used by the soil to facilitate the growth of plants and trees.

If the raindrop lands on a road, a rock, or any other hard surface, it simply runs off making no impact on where it landed.

The parable of the sower speaks of various receptacles of the seeds and how they were received. Some fell by the wayside and had no impact. Others fell on ground that benefited for a season, but then things got in the way. And some seeds fell on ground that was ready and willing to receive them for a lasting effect.

As I think about the rain outside my window, I begin to wonder about God's love. Isn't God's love kind of like those raindrops – we could call them love-drops. God's love-drops are raining down on us, and unlike the rain splattering on my skylight which will end at some point, there is no end to the love-drops of God. They are like an eternal shower of affection poured down on each and every one of us. They are constant, persistent, never ending.

But, what kind of surface do the love-drops of God find when they land? Is it soft, pliable, receptive? Does it have a positive impact on our lives? Or is the surface hard and repellant? Do we even notice the gentle dropping onto our lives? Too often His love-drops find my surface to be unresponsive. They just roll off.

Many things can get in the way of God's love-drops having an impact. Busyness, distractions, a myriad of diversions can interfere with the purpose God has for each love-drop.

It is this love that is raining down on us every moment of every day and every night. It is available to us whenever we need it. The ability to receive it – that is the battle.

This is the biggest struggle of my life – allowing the love of God to penetrate and have an impact. The counselor I saw after the death of Dr. Falwell was fighting his own battle with ALS. The last question I asked him before he succumbed to the disease was this. "Can we feel God's love?" His immediate response was an emphatic "Yes." I took that answer and made it my goal for the rest of my life to experience that love.

Letting go of the past is tough. I say this not as someone who is looking back and remembering what it was like, but as someone who is currently involved in the battle. The past refuses to go quietly into the night. It is like a leech that has a stranglehold on our lives and will not release its grip on us. At least, that's the way it is for me.

I go back to that dog that was wanting to come out from hiding and interact with the humans who were encouraging him. The dog inched its way partially from behind a wall, but then fear forced it back into safety. I am kind of like that with God. I want to praise Him, but there is still that force field energized by the issues of my past that get in the way. They are like a weight that drags on me.

During one of my counseling sessions, the counselor brought up the story about Peter walking on the water. He asked me what I thought Jesus' response was like when Peter told Him that he wanted to come to Jesus on the water. In other words, what was Jesus' demeanor? How did He react to the request?

After thinking for a second, I said that I envisioned Jesus being very ecclesiastical. By that I mean, I could see Him almost ceremoniously extend his hand out toward Peter, and in His best ministerial voice, with the tone of a sophisticated, refined cleric, say "Come".

My counselor then told me his concept of how Jesus responded to Peter. He thought that Jesus got really excited, put a big smile on his face, and in a voice that was enthusiastic and encouraging, invited Peter to "Come on out".

This question got right down to the issue of my life. Who is God? What is He really like? What emotions does He feel when He thinks about me? How much does He want me? Am I a passion of His, or just someone He tolerates? It's the intensity of God when dealing with me that I need to understand.

My main battle is with my knowledge of who God is and what motivates Him. As I have said, God was, and still is at times, standoffish, dispassionate, void of emotion when it comes to me. I have a hard time accepting God's love because, surely, I am not worthy of it. What is there in me that would cause God to really desire to have a relationship with me? Sometimes I feel like I need to do something before I can be counted worthy of God's love. Just being me doesn't even come close.

How is it possible for God to love me just the way I am? How can He be desirous of my prayers? Why would He care about all the little things in my life? What is His motivation? How excited is He to have me as His child?

This is the main battle of my life. Who is God? What is He like? Does He care about what's going on in the world? Even more than that, how much does He care? Is He intensely interested in the affairs of men, or is He just sitting up there in Heaven saying tsk, tsk, tsk, at the things He sees men doing. God loves us. How much? God cares about what's going on. How much? God is intervening in the lives of people. How passionate is He about that?

My question is not whether God involves Himself in the affairs of men, but to what extent His involvement is out of duty, or out of passion. How much does He crave the opportunities to show us Who He is?

This is my big struggle. My past keeps shouting at me. God does what He does because that's just who He is. It's just His character, and so any involvement in my life is simply God being God. He has no real desire, He just does it because that's who He is. There is no emotion involved, just a platonic performance of deeds on my behalf.

My past continues its rhetoric by pouncing on my belief that I am hardly someone who merits any consideration from God. I am a dud. I am not worth the effort. What could there possibly be about me that would cause God to take any notice? I don't stand out, I don't have any great talent to speak of, I certainly don't have a personality that would attract Him.

These are the thoughts that constantly drone on in my mind. They are entrenched. They are established patterns of thought. They are rooted and grounded in the experiences of my past, and the battle of my life is how to uproot what I've learned in the past and replace them with the truths of the present. It's hard because the lies of the past got a head start. The truth is Johnny-come-lately. The lies of the past have a long history in my life. The truth is just beginning the journey. The lies of the past will not just give up. But, neither will the truth of God. How to replace the lies of the past with the truth that never dies is the question.

I need to constantly look for opportunities to understand God. When I read the Bible, I must try to search for His character in the events and how God interacted with the people of those events. I must be open to things that God brings my way in everyday life that show me what He is like.

One December Sunday, I was sitting in the worship service at the end of one of the rows. Directly in front of me was a couple with a small baby in a carrier. They sat down and placed the carrier with the baby in it in the aisle right next to where they were sitting. I had the entire service to contemplate that child who was getting a head start in life by sleeping through the preaching.

Being December, I thought about Jesus being a baby. I thought about Jesus being this baby. It struck me just how helpless, how incapable, how dependent Jesus must have been when He was first born. I kept looking at the baby in front of me and envisioning Jesus in that exact form and marveling at how much Jesus humbled Himself to become someone so helpless. I went home that afternoon and wrote out the following:

> See the Son of God
>   Grasp for His first breath
>   Open His eyes to the world
>   Bawl when He is hungry
> He created the trees in the Garden for food, yet cries

out in hunger

See the Son of God
    Roll over on His stomach
    Learn how to crawl
    Take His first step
He was everywhere present, yet has to learn how to walk

See the Son of God
    Coo and goo
    Gurgle incoherent sounds
    Say His first word
He uttered the universe into existence, yet struggles to speak for the first time

See the Son of God
    Work with His hands
    Use tools of the trade
    In His daddy's shop
He created all that there is, yet learns to make things from what He created

See the Son of God
    Nailed to the cross
    Utter His last word
    Breathe His last breath
He created all life, yet dies a horrible death

When you see a child, imagine Jesus in that little body. Consider the limitations the Son of God placed upon Himself so that we could experience the limitless love and grace of God.

Jesus, the all-powerful, all knowing, everywhere present

Son of God, gave all that up to become a baby with no power, no knowledge, restricted in presence to this small body of a human baby. Why? Because He loved us with a love that defies description.

He didn't have to do this. It was His choice, a choice driven by love beyond all explanation.

The book of John has an interesting little twist to it. If my math is right, Jesus refers to His Father in Heaven 115 times in the first 19 chapters of the book. In every instance, at least in the NKJ English version, the article word in front of Father is either "the" or "my". It is always "the" Father, or "my" Father. That is, until chapter 20, verse 17. This is when Jesus was talking to Mary in the garden after the resurrection. Jesus said to her,

"Do not cling to Me, for I have not yet ascended to My Father; but go to My brethren and say to them, 'I am ascending to My Father AND YOUR FATHER, and to My God AND YOUR GOD.'"

I can't help but wonder if this might have been the most satisfying thing Jesus said during His entire ministry. He was acknowledging that His Father was no longer just His Father, He was now their Father, and our Father too. Jesus had finished what He came to accomplish. His mission was an unqualified success, and now He was able to proclaim His success to the very ones He redeemed.

At the last supper, Jesus expressed His feelings about eating this last Passover before He died with His disciples.

"When the hour had come, He sat down, and the twelve apostles with Him. Then He said to them, "With fervent desire I have desired to eat this Passover with you before I suffer; for I say to you, I will no longer eat of it until it is fulfilled in the kingdom of God."

It is my goal to constantly be open to things God shows me that reveal just how passionate He is when it comes to His relationship with me. I want to allow God's love-drops to find fertile and receptive soil when they land on me.

It's important to remember that if a love-drop lands on a hard, unresponsive surface, all is not lost. There is another drop right behind that one. The love of God never ends. It never runs out of steam. It bombards the surface of our lives relentlessly, it never gets discouraged, it never dissipates, it is one drop after another no matter what reception the previous drop got. The love-drops just keep on coming. There's no stopping them.

May we be receptive to who God is and allow the truth of His marvelous character to permeate deep down into the farthest depths of our lives. The more we expose ourselves to God, the more like Him we become. May that be the goal of our lives.

Made in the USA
Columbia, SC
14 September 2019